Sexuality

God's Gift

Edited by
Anne Krabill
Hershberger

Herald
Press

Scottdale, Pennsylvania
Waterloo, Ontario

Library of Congress Cataloging-in-Publication Data
Sexuality : God's Gift / edited by Anne Krabill Hershberger.
  p. cm.
  Includes bibliographical references.
  ISBN 0-8361-9111-0 (alk. paper)
  1. Sex instruction—Religious aspects—Mennonites. 2. Sex—Religious aspects—Mennonites. I. Hershberger, Anne Krabill, 1936- .
  HQ31.S515655 1999
  306.7—dc21   99-33721

The paper used in this publication is recycled and meets the minimum require-
ments of American National Standard for Information Sciences—Permanence
of Paper for Printed Library Materials, ANSI Z39.48-1984.

The form "Levels of Commitment" on page 131 may be copied for personal use.

SEXUALITY: GOD'S GIFT
Copyright © 1999 by Herald Press, Scottdale, Pa. 15683
  Published simultaneously in Canada by Herald Press,
  Waterloo, Ont. N2L 6H7. All rights reserved, except as noted above
Library of Congress Catalog Card Number: 99-33721
International Standard Book Number: 0-8361-9111-0
Printed in the United States of America
Cover and book design by Gwen M. Stamm
08 07 06 05 04 03 02 01 00 99 10 9 8 7 6 5 4 3 2 1

To order or request information, please call 1-800-759-4447
(individuals); 1-800-245-7894 (trade). Website: www.mph.org

Sexuality
God's Gift

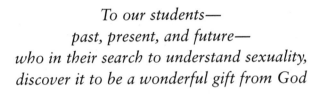

To our students—
past, present, and future—
who in their search to understand sexuality,
discover it to be a wonderful gift from God

Contents

Foreword by J. Lawrence Burkholder 9
Preface 11
Acknowledgments 13

1. The Gift 15
   Anne Krabill Hershberger and Willard S. Krabill

2. Guidelines from the Gift-Giver:
   Sexuality and Scripture 33
   Keith Graber Miller

3. The Gift and Intimacy 49
   Willard S. Krabill

4. The Gift and Young People 62
   Michael A. Carrera and Anne Krabill Hershberger

5. The Gift and Singleness 71
   From *Human Sexuality in the Christian Life*

6. The Gift and Marriage 83
   Willard S. Krabill

7. The Gift and Same-Sex Orientation 99
   Willard S. Krabill

8. The Gift and Cross-Gender Friendships 118
   Willard S. Krabill

9. The Gift and the Sensuous 126
   Anne Krabill Hershberger

10. The Gift Expressed in the Arts 134
    Lauren Friesen

11. The Gift Misused 149
    Willard S. Krabill and Anne Krabill Hershberger
12. The Gift Restored 172
    Delores Histand Friesen
13. The Gift: Further Study 191
    *Delores Histand Friesen and
    Anne Krabill Hershberger*

Notes 204
Contributing Authors 209

Foreword

BY CREATING THEM male and female (Gen. 1:27), God introduced the principle of sexuality into the physical world. Along with the force of gravity and the speed of light, the mutual attraction of the sexes became a law of nature. Scientists have noticed that the proton and the neutron at the center of the atom are mysteriously attracted to each other by the strongest force of nature, analogous to the relation of the sexes. At any rate, sexuality is a broadly based given of the natural world. As a general principle, it may be said that where there is life, there is sex.

Since sexuality is a given of the created order, how can it be experienced as a "gift" of God's grace? That is the question addressed in this significant book. Any historical examination of sexuality would indicate that the relation between the sexes is complex. The very duality of male and female differentiation contains within itself the possibility of both joyful and even ecstatic union, or of discordant conflict. As everyone knows, some sexual unions are happy and others are disastrous. Yet when experienced as a gift of God's grace, sexuality may be described as "one flesh" (Mark 10:8), a unity that portents the restoration of all things, when God shall be "all in all" (1 Cor. 15:28).

This book is not a sex manual. It is not about the rudiments of sexual relations, though these are not ignored. It is an interpretation of sexuality from the perspective of its multiple dimensionality. Sexuality is seen in relationship to facets of life that, when examined separately, are called psychology, sociology, medicine, spirituality, philosophy, and theology. Unique to this volume is the manner in which these dimensions have been

9

brought to bear upon sexuality in its broader applications. This is really a philosophy of sexuality seen from a Christian perspective.

Though this is a collection of essays featuring different aspects of sexuality, I see no evidence of major disagreement among its contributors. Since it represents a point of view, special credit should go to the major contributions of Dr. Willard Krabill and his sister Anne Krabill Hershberger, editor, who have researched human sexuality for many years. At Goshen College, Dr. Krabill originated the course on "Human Sexuality" and taught it for 17 years. That course has received the acclamation of students and has also left a legacy of constructive Christian ideas and attitudes, to benefit future generations and the Mennonite Church.

Dr. Krabill's chapter on same-sex orientation should be required reading for those who want to know what can be known and what cannot be known about this controversial subject. Anne collaborates with Willard and the other contributors to set forth a common point of view about such relevant aspects of sexuality as intimacy, singleness, marriage, friendship, community, healing, and sensuous experience.

Who should benefit from this book? The answer is, everyone—whether directly or indirectly. Parents, pastors, Sunday school teachers, young people, counselors, couples, singles, and grandparents will do well to examine sexuality from the standpoint of critical examination of historic attitudes, the modern "sexual revolution," and biblical scholarship. If twelve-year-old adolescents cannot be expected to sit still long enough to read it through, they can still benefit indirectly by the enlightened attitudes of their elders. After all, to be human is to be sexual.

Sexuality has become a dominant theme in popular culture. Hence, Christians need to review this important dimension of life as understood scientifically, discussed honestly, examined sympathetically, interpreted theologically, and presented humbly.

—*J. Lawrence Burkholder, President Emeritus*
  Goshen College

Preface

Can there be anything more to write about human sexuality than what has already appeared in existing literature? Each year new textbooks are published with updated content. Popular bookstores devote increasing amounts of shelf space to books related to sexuality. Information on sexuality is found through the computer Internet and creative audiovisual media. Pornography, a distortion of sexuality, continues each year as a multibillion-dollar industry.

Research reports in many fields of study show how sexuality issues are related to the concerns of those disciplines. In recent years more people with faith and religious perspectives have shared their thinking and study regarding sexuality. Literature on sexuality has been written for all age groups. So what special purpose does this book attempt to fulfill?

The conception of this book began more than a decade ago when Delores Histand Friesen approached Willard S. Krabill about collaborating on a sexuality volume written from a Christian perspective. Such a book would complement excellent secular texts used by students in the sexuality classes Delores was teaching at Mennonite Brethren Biblical Seminary (Fresno, California) and Willard at Goshen (Indiana) College.

As years passed, Delores and Willard continued to believe in the importance of this project, but neither found time to give leadership to it. Willard was writing and speaking throughout the Mennonite Church about living whole lives and respecting God's good gift of sexuality. In 1991 he retired from teaching the sexuality course he had originated at Goshen College in

1973. It was always a popular course. He had developed extensive resources, class and speech notes, and publications that seemed appropriate to adapt for the book envisioned.

After Willard's retirement from teaching, I, his sister, associate professor of nursing at Goshen College, began to team-teach the sexuality course, first with Thomas J. Meyers, professor of sociology; and later with Keith Graber Miller, associate professor of Bible, religion, and philosophy. It became clear to me that a book such as Delores and Willard had discussed would be quite useful in the course.

In 1996 I was granted a sabbatical leave for one year and met with Willard and Delores to discuss the future for this book. A decision was made to move forward with the project. My sabbatical schedule made it possible for me to begin editing and writing. I combined and edited some of the good work already prepared and enhanced it by adding some new material.

This book is not intended to be an exhaustive treatise nor the last word on the topic of sexuality. To help us understand the field, many textbooks present thorough and research-based findings, charts, illustrations, and descriptive narratives. This volume instead is an attempt to put in accessible form some topics on sexuality that have special meanings for Christians and to interpret them from a Christian, Anabaptist, biblical perspective. This is the current thinking of several persons who have spent many years studying these issues, want to further the discussion, and who care deeply about reflecting Christian values in life.

We hope this book will be useful as a complement to the secular sexuality textbooks in sexuality classes on Christian campuses. It may also serve as a resource for small discussion groups and Sunday school classes in congregational settings.

To fulfill these purposes, the book has been organized by headings keyed to the metaphor of sexuality as a gift from God. Each chapter offers questions to help stimulate group discussion. Chapter 13 lists resources for further study. The notes provide documentation, arranged by chapters and authors' names.

The book is meant to provide help for both individuals and groups. The authors desire that each reader will perceive healthy sexuality as vital to human wholeness, intimacy, joy, and caring relationships, as well as a reflection of God's creative love.

The chapter contributors are Christian educators who also have professional roles such as physician, nurse, theologian, counselor, and dramatist. We believe it has been worthwhile to bring all of these perspectives together for further educating readers about sexuality. We trust the readers will agree.

—*Anne Krabill Hershberger*
Goshen College

Acknowledgments

THE SUCCESS of any work of this kind depends on the cooperation and goodwill of the collaborators. I am especially grateful for the continual support and helpful suggestions of my brother, Willard Krabill, the primary contributor to this book. He made his past materials on sexuality available to me for updating and editing. He willingly changed some of his former writing and added new content as needed. Willard reviewed several drafts, believed in this project, and helped it come to fruition in many ways.

The other contributors are Delores Histand Friesen, Keith Graber Miller, and Lauren Friesen. They brought their unique and significant interpretations and experiences to expand and facilitate better understanding of sexuality from a Christian perspective.

As a project for the "Human Sexuality" course in the fall of 1997, a group of six students at Goshen College volunteered to read the book's content as written to that point. They critiqued it from their points of view as college students. Their comments and suggestions were extremely helpful, and many of them were incorporated in the final draft. These students were Sonia Gingerich, Keith Herris, Matthew Martin, Annie

Mininger, Grant Rissler, and Amanda Yoder. My teaching colleague, Keith Graber Miller, graciously consented to critique the students' projects to assure greater objectivity. He gave me helpful suggestions on that early draft of the book. The staff at Herald Press constructively contributed to the final shaping of the book.

Many friends, associates, and church leaders who heard about the project were encouraging and eager to see the finished product. This provided helpful stimulation to continue.

I appreciate the Mennonite Church and the General Conference Mennonite Church for granting me permission to reprint with minor editing a section from the 1985 working document *Human Sexuality in the Christian Life.* I also thank Michael A. Carrera for permission to reprint a chapter from his book *Lessons for Lifeguards: Working with Teens When the Topic Is Hope.*

My family was supportive of this project in so many ways. They are my husband, Abner; my daughters, Kay and Sue; Kay's husband, Brian Burnett; and Sue's husband, Jon Yoder. Brian's computer consultation was quite helpful in bringing this project to completion.

To all of these persons, I say a deep-felt thank you.

—*Anne Krabill Hershberger*

1

The Gift

Anne Krabill Hershberger and Willard S. Krabill

WHAT IS IT about a gift that is so appealing? The very fact that *someone has given me a gift* is a gift in and of itself. Someone thought enough of me to prepare a gift. Surely the *presentation* is part of the appeal. Gifts come in a variety of forms, of course. Often bright-colored paper and ribbons show that something special is being presented. Sometimes there is just a word, picture, or brown butcher paper in the presentation.

Often there is *mystery*—what could it be? We enthusiastically and literally tear into a package or gently handle the gift so we will not damage any part of it. Then we discover what a person who cares for us thought would bring us pleasure.

True gifts are *pleasurable*. The gift may be something in line with our interests, with a good fit, or a pleasing color. It may be an item, event, resource, or word that is so helpful or delightful, and yet we might never think to buy it or be able to get it for ourselves. It may be a humor-packed something that keeps us laughing every time we think of it. The gift might be a thoughtful gesture that can come only from someone who really knows what we are dealing with in our lives. A gift brings pleasure in so many ways.

So why is our sexuality being named a *gift* from God? If we compare it with the characteristics of gifts mentioned above, we think about the fact that God chose to make us sexual, both alike as people and different in gender, but each of us as a sexual being. Sexuality has been given to us. It is here, with us, a gift. It is key in making us who we are.

This gift also is inherent in our *presentation*. From the earliest moments of conception and embryological development, while God was knitting each of us together in the mother's womb (Ps. 139:13), our sexuality was established, determining our gender. When presented to our parents, we were a newborn baby girl or boy and all that represents. No bright paper or bows accompanied our presentation. Yet there certainly was an excitement and expectation that there was a new life in either male or female form. Each of us was a new person with potential to make a difference in the world in a unique way.

The *mystery* of our sexuality is present throughout life. Infants touch and explore their own body parts. They thrive only when older human beings touch, cuddle, coo, gaze upon, rock, carry, and sing and talk to them. During preschool years, children solve the mystery of whether they are girls or boys. No amount of teasing or arguing will talk them out of their determination.

As a child enters the school-age years, many developmental tasks require attention, but permeating everything else is the mystery of sexuality: "Why am I like I am?" "Where did I come from?" "Am I normal?" "What is right for me to be doing as a girl or as a boy?" This interest in and exploration of the mystery of sexuality is right there all of the time.

When people enter puberty, they "tear into the package" or, in fear and trembling, respond to the bombardment of sexual thoughts, images, and feelings coming from within and without. For many people, trying to understand the mystery of sexuality at this time of life almost becomes a preoccupation.

As we move into adulthood and throughout our middle and older years, we have the potential to gain greater insights into the mystery and to experience the mature richness of our sexuality. We realize that sexuality refers to all those parts of the human personality and body that collectively identify us as male or female. Sexuality is not just genital sex or sexual intercourse. Always, from birth to death, we all are sexual beings.

The gift of sexuality, like other gifts, is meant to be a source of *pleasure* in our lives. This pleasure is expressed poetically by Solomon's Song of Songs in the Bible: "How much more pleasing is your love than wine, and the fragrance of your perfume than any spice!" (4:10b). The marriage at Cana was a cause for celebration as well as the occasion for Jesus' first recorded miracle, turning water into wine (John 2:1-11). Throughout, the Bible gives a clear message that love should permeate relationships of all kinds and bring the greatest of pleasures. Of course, all of these relationships are formed by sexual people.

As Christian adults, we do not believe that things "just happen." We believe in a God who has created the world, orderly and predictable, and we are a part of that creation. It is predictable that if we transgress God's design for our lives, we will have to pay a price. Our right decisions about our sexuality today can bless our future days tremendously. Our wrong decisions about our uses of and purposes in sex today can blight our tomorrows in many ways. Later in this book, we will discuss these right and wrong decisions related to sexuality.

To build our gift of sexuality into an optimally healthy sexuality, we must carefully lay a proper foundation. To do so, we identify and discuss specific foundation stones needed for this important grounding.

Theology of the Body

The first foundation stone for a healthy sexuality is a proper theology of the body, a proper system of belief about our bodies. Over the centuries a false belief has crept into our thinking, suggesting that the body is evil and the spirit is good. Somehow we have grown up thinking that it is wrong to enjoy and feel good about our bodies—really about ourselves, for in our bodies we are ourselves.

We say we believe in the wholeness of persons; that we are body, mind, and spirit; and that preaching, teaching, and healing are all valid ministries. We talk about holistic health concepts. Yet in our churches, we seem to recognize only the spirit. Too often in our colleges, we recognize only the intellect and regard a good academic record as far more important than a proper heart rate, a needed weight loss, or a fitness score.

A circle, not a triangle, is a better presentation of this concept of the human organism. We are integrated and continuous whole beings, not isolated sides held together. By separating our physical selves from our minds and spirits, we too easily go right on overeating, overworking, overdrinking, overdriving our cars, and overspending time in sitting around and spectating. Nowhere is our failure to have a proper attitude toward our bodies more damaging to us than in relation to our sexuality.

Sexually speaking, if my body is evil and not really "me," then I cannot be held responsible for the wrong things my body does. I may try to excuse myself: "I just couldn't help it. I had this overwhelming passion." James B. Nelson says in *Embodiment* (see Notes) that when my body ceases to be fully personal, my relationships to other body-selves are diminished. If *my* body is not good and fully me, then neither is *your* body anything I need to hold sacred. I can more easily use your body or abuse mine. Subtle thoughts and inferences can run in that direction.

Our false thinking about the body also keeps us from speaking openly and honestly about our sexual bodies. We are often reluctant and even ashamed to talk about them. It is amazing how many married couples have slept together for years and have even raised a family, yet not once have they been able to talk with each other about their bodies. Not once have these couples spoken about pleasuring their bodies, about their sexual lives, or about their sexual feelings and preferences.

Having a proper theology of the body would lead us to feel exuberant about the way our bodies allow us to express ourselves, enjoy a wide variety of sensations, reach out to others in fostering relationships, experience this good creation, and reflect the image of God. This is surely a gift.

Sexual Theology

The second foundation stone, a proper sexual theology, follows closely and naturally. Do we really believe and understand that sex is good, and that our sexuality is a good gift from God? God could have arranged for us to reproduce in another way, but he chose to create us the way we are. How does the church view the meaning of sex?

The church should have a truly Christian attitude in educating about sexuality, in our witness to the world, and in our practice. Of all people, we as believers ought to have the most positive attitude toward our bodies and toward our sexuality. We are the ones who know the God who made them. We who know God best should best reflect the true nature of human sexuality.

How then does it happen that today we allow those who do not know the Creator of our sexuality to define sexuality, to determine what is true or untrue, and to set our sexual standards? We have permitted some harmful misconceptions and false attitudes to creep into our thinking about sexuality. As a result, we do not have a good track record in dealing with those who are hurting in this area of their lives.

We Christians need to put our sexual stance, message, and practice in tune with the Creator of human sexuality, and then spread that true word and become visible in the debate. Let the message become loud and clear that our sexuality is a source of true joy, healing, love, caring, and unselfishness. It is not the source of misery, hurt, and pain so often caused by people misusing sexuality.

Let us read the Bible, expecting to find a positive message about human sexuality. It is there. We have read everything else; so here we might observe, "When all else fails, read the directions." In the Bible we will find an affirmation of gender differences, a blessing from God when we allow love to permeate our relationships, and a sense that each individual is valuable—as a sexual person.

Respect for Males and Females

A third foundation stone in building healthy sexuality is a proper understanding of respect for males and females. In spite of all our scientific knowledge, we don't fully understand—biologically, developmentally, and physiologically—how alike males and females are. Where we are not alike, we are either equal or complementary. There should be no room for a double standard in Christian circles.

Nevertheless, we have a long way to go in understanding proper male-female roles, responsibilities, and expectations. Black leaders tell us that America is never so racially segregated as it is on Sunday morning. It is likely also true that America is never so sexist as it is on Sunday morning. Paternalistic attitudes are frequently apparent in some church settings. If we really believe that God has created us sexual, male and female, and that each is of equal value and unable to exist without the other, we will have difficulty giving hierarchical value to the genders.

We are all exposed to less-than-ideal views of the other sex. This apparently starts early in life. A classroom teacher asked the children to write anything they pleased about people. A little pigtailed girl wrote, "People are composed of two kinds, boys and girls. Boys are no good at all until they grow up and get married. Boys are an awful bother. They want everything but soap. A woman is a grown-up girl with children. My dad is such a nice man that I am sure he must have been a little girl when he was a boy." This little girl's last comment reveals a truth that many adults would do well to note: ideally, male and female attributes are found in all of us.

It is apparent that respect in male-female relationships is lacking when one notes a "scoring," aggressor-conquest mentality. This communicates an attitude of overpowering others instead of mutual respect. Such an attitude or a male-infallibility complex tends to block marital communication and marital counseling efforts. In effect, the man says, "Problem? I've got no problem. *She's* the one who has the problem." Too many men cannot understand how any sexual problem in a marriage could be the male's fault.

Young people sometimes experience a double standard when exposed to the attitudes of those who excuse inappropriate male sexual behavior by saying, "Boys will be boys." Females in this same situation are often referred to as "loose," "sluts," or worse. Such responses do not demonstrate respect.

If we have true respect for each other as males and females, that can help us to be comfortable in each other's presence, share common interests and concerns on many levels, and develop a genuine concern for others. We can bring out the best in each other's behavior, consciously recognize the fundamental way in which we are part of each other, and find joy in our relationships. Individuals thrive best in community, not in isolation. Our own sexuality is enhanced by honoring and respecting the sexuality of others. Promoting this kind of respect is worthy of great effort on the part of each of us.

Integration of Sex and Life

The fourth foundation stone for healthy sexuality is the understanding that our sexuality is an integral part of who we are. It reaches through our whole life. As mentioned earlier, we—all of the time—are sexual beings. All of the time we communicate as sexual beings. Our sexuality is that pervasive essence of our personality that forever and every time defines us first as humans and second as males or females.

We always relate to others as sexual persons, but that does not mean we necessarily have genital sex in mind. Genital sexual intercourse is only one part of sexuality. A person can be a whole, healthy, fulfilled, and vibrantly sexual being without ever experiencing genital intercourse. Our sexuality is who we are, not what we do. Sex is not a compartment of our lives and beings that we can treat separately.

Let us compare the different styles of integrating and compartmentalizing our lives, as sometimes seen in the marital sexual relationship. A successful sexual experience begins when the married couple gets up in the morning. The attitudes, the caring, the tenderness, and the messages communicated all day —whether outwardly about finances, the children's lessons, the in-laws, the cold soup, or the soggy pie crust—are all the prelude to yet another message, a message of "love."

In another scenario, two people may fight, nag, scold, argue, put down, or ignore all day and all evening—and then expect great things to happen in bed at night. Such inconsistency does not make sense.

Marriage counselors estimate that when couples present themselves for help with sexual problems, 80 percent of the time the problem is not sexual. It may be about finances, a clothing allowance, in-laws, tension and dissension over disciplining the children, personal hygiene, or many other conflicts. Because of these stresses in the marriage, the sexual relationship suffers and often gets the blame.

Our bodies should say the same thing the rest of our being is saying; otherwise we live a lie. If I say "I'm yours" with my body when it is not true in reality, that is dishonest, destructive, and inexcusable.

Affirming the Sexuality of All People

The fifth foundation stone is the affirmation of the sexuality of *all* people. Many people show that this stone is missing by denying the sexuality of their parents. This denial may run like this: "Sex is dirty; my parents are nice people; therefore my parents are not sexual." Our presence in the world is effective testimony that this denial is ill-founded.

We cannot and should not deny the sexuality of anyone— whether male or female, young or old, parents or children, ill or well, handicapped or those without visible handicaps, mentally brilliant or dull, married or single.

In his excellent book, *The Sexual Celibate,* Donald Goergen promotes a valid concept, strange as it may seem:

> A celibate person is not asexual. He or she has a full sexual life which needs to be understood in order to have a richer understanding of Christian sexuality itself as well as in order to assist people in living a celibate life. . . . The sexual life of a celibate person is going to manifest itself primarily in the affective bonds of permanent and steadfast human friendships which are exemplifications of God's way of loving. Through a rediscovery of friendship within the Christian tradition and through an integration of community, friendship, ministry, and prayer, the present discussion of celibacy can lead to a revival of a truly Christian value, the value of friendship, which is a service for the entire Christian community. (224-225)

When we affirm the sexuality of all people, we include older people. We tend to desexualize seniors. It is false to assume that they have no sexual feelings, no sexual needs, and no need for affection. A passage from the book *Sexuality and the Sacred,* edited by James B. Nelson and Sandra P. Longfellow, comments pertinently on "Older Adults":

> Faithfulness to the gracious God who has created us for wholeness requires that we affirm . . . the possibility of securing sexual justice for older adults, of transforming relationships, of reclaiming God's gift of eros for persons of all ages. As sexual beings, we require and reach out for the physical and spiritual embrace of others. As Christians, we seek to make such embrace possible for all persons by securing right relatedness and the concrete well-being of individuals and communities. (301-302)

The general population often denies or ignores the sexuality of another large group of people, the disabled. What able-bodied people's attitudes have done to the disabled is unconscionable. Christians cannot permit it to continue. "To desex someone is profoundly to dehumanize that person" (Nelson: 212).

People with all types of disabilities continue to have interest in sexuality and sexual expression. They may have nonprogressive physical disabilities such as blindness, amputation, or spinal cord injury; progressive physical disabilities such as cystic fibrosis and multiple sclerosis; or a serious illness or mental retardation.

"Regardless of the degree of physical incapacitation, if there is consciousness there is still self-awareness of one's masculinity and femininity, one's body image, one's desire and need for intimate human relatedness" (Nelson: 217). The development of creative and satisfying means of sexual expression has brought pleasure and true intimacy to many disabled people and those with whom they relate.

When persons are mentally retarded, special individualized approaches to sexuality education must be devised to communicate in meaningful ways. Concerns regarding contraception, sterilization, marriage, and parenting must be faced realistically. Many mentally disabled people are sexually abused. They need special protection because they may not be able to recognize when they are particularly vulnerable to this kind of relationship. Whatever the special needs of the mentally disabled, "they share with the rest of us the basic human interests in closeness, affection, physical contact, and simply being in on things" (Nelson: 228).

The disabled need advocates who can help to raise consciousness and to legitimize their sexuality and need for close human contacts and sexual expression.

Sound Sex Education

The sixth stone necessary to build a foundation for healthy sexuality is sound sex education. Our understandings about human sexuality and our sexual attitudes are learned. They need to be communicated by the best teachers available. Sound sex education is imperative for a happy, safe, and positive sexual destiny.

Loving, affectionate, and communicating parents are basic necessities in a sound sex education program. They must be able to talk about their sexuality with ease and candor, and their own sexual lifestyle must be Christian.

A second element is a caring and loving faith community. The church that ignores or does not speak about the subject of sexuality indirectly communicates that sexuality does not warrant a place on the Christian education agenda. The church group is (at least theoretically) best equipped to educate children, young people, and adults alike about sexuality. Church members know the Creator of our sexuality. We presume to have a growing knowledge and understanding of the Bible, the primary textbook on how to live life abundantly and as whole people. We care about modeling the spiritual values upheld in the Bible.

Our young people are receiving sex education every day. Nevertheless, we wonder, "What kind?"

Ideally, sex education begins in the home with loving parents, and sexual modeling certainly takes place there. Many parents, however, are still embarrassed or insecure with their own sexual feelings and their ability to talk about sexuality. This makes it hard for them to open up the subject with their children.

Schools can provide some knowledge and counseling, but children need more emphasis on spiritual values related to sexuality than many schools are permitted or able to provide. Children need a foundation in sexuality with spiritual values before they experience the onslaught of hedonistic mass media influences or are passionately involved themselves.

The church is ideally suited to model, interpret, and promote a spiritual frame of reference for sexuality.

Whatever the setting for spiritually sound sex education, the messages communicated must be accurate, clearly defined, developmentally and culturally appropriate, and pertinent to the students. The basic message is that our sexuality is a good gift from God and is given for our pleasure. We must also include the message that in growing up sexually, each person needs to establish her or his identity before becoming physically intimate with another person. On all sides, we see tragic results when young people have experienced sexual intercourse before they have found their own identities.

Another important message is that sexuality is far more than anatomy, physiology, and the sexual response system. It is most of all a matter of communication, relationship, and commitment.

Whatever else can be said about sexual intercourse, it is never casual, even though some would treat it so. Our popular culture proclaims that so-called casual sex is nothing but fun, nothing but freedom, nothing but this or that—no big deal. Yet my experience as a physician with many patients and college students reveals that it *is* a big deal. Some consider it as casual as sharing a Coke or holding hands, but their sexual behavior exhibits a monstrous denial of their basic humanity. Their behavior is crude and animalistic and does not show *human* sexuality—not in its character and not in its potential.

Sex is not individualistic, not a "do your own thing" kind of activity. Some have the notion that the decisions a young couple makes about sexual lifestyle are of no concern to anyone else. That is not true. Henry Fairlie put this into perspective:

There is no more pat shibboleth of our time than the idea that what consenting adults do in private is solely their own business. That is false. What we do in private has repercussions on ourselves; and what we are and believe has repercussions on others. What we do in our own homes will inevitably affect, not only our own behavior outside them, but also what we expect and tolerate in the behavior of others. A change in manners or discipline in the family will not leave unchanged the manners and discipline in the wider society. When we recognize how deeply our sexual feelings are registers of our whole beings, it is mere trifling to say that our societies ought not to be constantly alert to the manner in which we employ them. (20)

Sound sex education promotes a broader understanding of the term *good-looking* than the usual definition. In our media, "good-looking" and "sexy" tend to get intertwined with each other. Hence, to be "good-looking" usually means to be "sexy" or at least sexually appealing, never mind one's character, thoughtfulness, loyalty, generosity, values—all of which enhance one's attractiveness. Striving for what the world considers "good looks" can become an obsession when "good looks" are defined in terms of handsome faces, shapely legs, thigh proportion, hairy chests, or bust measurements. Such ratings ignore the personal worth of many people.

Our culture has prescribed for women an image of female beauty that does not fit healthy physiology. It is contrary to what normally happens as women mature. Thus the majority are automatically consigned to the ranks of the "not good looking." The desire for thinness and unrealistic body image is one of the pernicious factors that has made eating disorders, such as anorexia and bulimia, major problems with young North American women today. The false value assigned to physical good looks is one of the prime characteristics of our culture.

Celebration of Sex

The last foundation stone for a healthy sexuality is that sexuality is to be celebrated.

How does God recommend that we celebrate our sexuality?

The first and greatest commandment given sets the tone for all the other recommendations: " 'Love the Lord your God with all your heart and with all your soul and with all your mind.' . . . And the second is like it: 'Love your neighbor as yourself' " (Matt. 22:37, 39). Adherence to these two commandments could remove the need for any other recommendations. If we truly loved God and loved our neighbors as ourselves, we would treat others as we would like to be treated.

"While the Bible does not spell out a detailed theory of sex, it does . . . open up for us a perspective on life as a whole, including our sexuality," says Neil Clark Warren. Our beliefs regarding human wholeness and personhood are derived from biblical truth, and the Bible has a high and celebrative view of sexuality.

The following descriptions show what living a celebrative life as sexual people at each stage of life could be like:

• As *infants and children*, we are loved, protected, and nourished. We are stimulated to learn and develop. We are humored but also have appropriate limits set for us. We do not need to be warned about or experience inappropriate touching or sexual behavior by family members, relatives, neighbors, "friends," or strangers. We can safely explore the wonderful world of nature, science, and art at any time, inside or outside.

• As *preadolescents and adolescents*, we continue to experience the security of an intact, loving family. They have the good sense to know when to reach out, and when to allow privacy, but are always there to help interpret life and our concerns about growing up. Our life's experiences include school programs, teachers, and classmates that stimulate us to become the best we can be. We go to schools that make learning fun in a safe environment and that augment positive sexual learning from home. We are part of a church and community that cares about spiritual development and creates many wholesome, fun activities where we can be with our peers, try out our social skills, and experience the satisfaction of doing things together that are helpful to other people. We are not mercilessly teased as we experience the stirrings of sexual attractions.

• *As young adults*, the disciplines and patterns of living and thinking established earlier serve us well as we continue our education and explore options in living arrangements, work, and friends. We gain a clear sense of who we are becoming and like what we see. Our choices regarding lifestyle, singleness, marriage, and geographical location give us feelings of satisfaction and fulfillment. As women or men, we can feel accepted and appreciated for who we are. We are seen as people of character rather than as sexual objects. We live where no man or woman will dread going to work because of co-workers' use of verbal and body language laden with sexual innuendoes, and where going for a walk morning, noon, or night feels safe. We know that a date means a fun opportunity to learn to know another person better—not an invitation to sleep together. We want a world where it is not necessary for any of us to figure out how to tell the person we hope to marry about a sexually transmitted disease that will always be with us. We want to be free of the need to discuss sexual partners in the past, a child born out of wedlock, or an abortion. We want to be free of the need to explain that we were sexually abused and raped and therefore will need a lot of sensitive understanding before it will be possible for us to feel comfortable with sexual intercourse.

• *As adults*, we find that the choices we have made contribute to a sense of great personal satisfaction as well as the knowledge that we make a positive difference in the lives of others. We who remain single find significant social interaction and support from caring friends of both genders, opportunities for both receiving and contributing in important ways in church and community settings, and freedom from sexual harassment. We who marry experience open and clear communication and can learn with our spouses what is pleasurable to each in our sexual relationship without feeling we are being compared with previous partners. Children are viewed as gifts from God, for whom we joyfully assume responsibility. We who want children can have them. We offer hospitality in our homes to many others. Learning and spiritual development are a continuing process, and service is a way of everyday life.

• *As older adults*, we enjoy the results of a life that is and has been well-lived and filled with wise choices and adventure. We experience companionship with family and friends from all age ranges as well as acceptance, tender care, and desired touching. We are offered spiritual resources to help us cope with the growing number of losses older people inevitably experience. We continue to focus on people and events beyond ourselves and contribute to improving the lives of others as possible. A life lived according to God's design prepares us for a joyful entrance into eternal life.

Do these descriptions of life at every stage sound like heaven? They are a bit of heaven. After all, Christ indicated that he came to earth that we might have life, and have it to the full (John 10:10). The whole biblical story is about relationships— human beings' relationships to God, to each other, to themselves, to family members, to brothers and sisters in Christ, to orphans and widows, to "the least of these," and to enemies. In all of these relationships, the people interacting are doing so as sexual beings. They cannot do otherwise, since to be human is to be sexual.

We also know that these interactions are occurring in imperfect societies made up of people with flaws. God knows this, of course. He has provided principles and guidelines in the Bible to help us deal with what is less than ideal in the human experience, recognize the temptations that fight against living life abundantly as God would have us do, and pattern our lives in the way God would have us live.

For people in biblical times, God prescribed principles on which to base attitudes and behavior. Our culture is quite different from that of biblical societies. Yet the same principles are just as appropriate for us today. Living as sexual beings while following God's way truly does lead to the most rewarding, satisfying, healthy, uncomplicated, freeing, nurturing, and intimate life possible. Even in an imperfect world, God's recommendations for human interaction can help to prevent the pain, grief, destruction, and unfulfilled dreams that so often occur when people yield to selfish, undisciplined, and unloving attitudes in their sexual interactions.

Sexuality is for rejoicing; sexuality can be a source of happiness; sexuality should mean fulfillment. How beautiful that sexuality was created as a dimension of God's highest creation.

We realize a sense of peace and true sexual freedom when we are part of a community that honors our sexuality and our uniqueness, that frees us from compulsive genital expression and preoccupation, and that shows us how to trust each other. We can only imagine what would happen if the male half of the human race and the female half of the human race could achieve true peace with each other, living together in harmony, equality, love, mutual respect, and honor. Both individual peace and world peace would be remarkably enhanced.

Someone has said that those who are mentally and emotionally healthy are those who have learned to say three things: when to say, "yes," when to say, "no," and when to say, "whoopee!" Our sexuality can be one of the whoopees of our lives—a very special gift from God.

Discussion Questions

1. What are some examples of false thinking about the body that keeps us from
   • speaking openly and honestly about our sexual bodies?
   • reaching out to others to foster relationships?
2. Are my attitudes about sexuality the same as or different from how I perceive my parents' or guardians' attitudes? Why?

3. How might Christian attitudes and understandings of sexuality be made more visible in our society?

4. If we truly believe that God created us sexual, male and female, and that each is of equal value and unable to exist without the other, what changes might we observe in our congregations, institutions, families, and interpersonal relationships?

5. Identify and explain how you might develop
   • male attributes you as a female would like to possess to a greater extent.
   • female attributes you as a male would like to possess to a greater extent.

6. If you were to design an ideal sex education program in your congregation, what would it be?

2

Guidelines from the Gift-Giver
Sexuality and Scripture

Keith Graber Miller

IN SEXUALITY, as in all areas of our lives, our ethical discernment and understandings are rooted in multiple sources, including but not limited to the biblical text. Once I heard about a Sunday school class that was studying the matter of women in church leadership.

The teacher began by saying he wanted everyone, on entering the room, to leave their "baggage" at the door. He wanted them to set aside their preconceptions about the issue, their social locations, their gender, their life experiences, their education, ideas from their culture, and all other notions that had shaped them. With that baggage discarded, the teacher said, they would simply look at the Bible and see what the unadulterated Scripture had to say to them on the issue.

When I learned of that approach, I thought, "What a horrendous deception! It's impossible to leave all these things at the door." Instead, when I teach, I want people to bring their baggage with them. Together we can place the baggage on the floor in front of us and open it. It will take time to sort through the luggage, unpacking, laundering, repacking, and shifting. We will throw out some of the muck—the soiled underwear and maybe those dreadful bellbottom jeans from the '70s (or the '90s). We will exchange or share some of our finer articles with others. We will try to make everything fit a little better. But we will not get anywhere with any integrity if we do not see how much we are shaped by all of these other factors, and

if we do not begin to accept the impact of those other forma-
tive influences.

In our understandings of sexuality, most of us, implicitly or
explicitly, draw on our own experiences and those of our parents, siblings, friends, work associates, and church family. We
consider the sciences; we ask what contemporary social and
natural scientists are saying about genetics, biological predis-
positions, and social construction of our sexual desires, incli-
nations, and perspectives. We examine what seems "natural" or
"unnatural," based on the way God has apparently ordered the
world. For some Christians, these other sources function as independent "authorities" alongside the Bible. For others, they are
interpretive lenses through which we look at the biblical text.

We also ask how the church—the larger church or our own
denomination—has weighed in on a given issue over the centuries. In doing so, we need to acknowledge that the living tradition has developed and changed over the ages. In addition, we
should recognize how our views of the Bible itself have been
shaped by the church's tradition in ways we often overlook.

Augustine of Hippo (354-430), one of the most influential
early church theologians, had a profound impact on the
church's views of sex and sexuality. Before he committed himself to Christian faith, he had a rather active youth. He fa-
thered a child outside of marriage, lived with a woman, and
constantly struggled with his sexual impulses. After his con-
version and as he processed his personal experience, Augustine
and some of his peers decided that it was coitus, and more
specifically the male erection, that showed the will's inability
to maintain control over the passions. Such uncontrollability
was a major concern for those concerned that one's "spiritual
nature" should control one's "physical nature."

Augustine also linked the act of sexual intercourse with the
transmission of original sin. Since such sin was handed on
from generation to generation and since future generations
were created through coitus, genital-genital intercourse be-

came inextricably linked with original sin.

Over the centuries, the Christian tradition developed into what some critics disparagingly call a "sex-negative" one. I would like to believe that is not true. But even *if,* by some measures, the Christian *tradition* is a sex-negative one, the *Bible itself* is not.

Hebrew Scriptures

From the beginning of the Hebrew Scriptures (Old Testament), sex and sexuality are considered good. In the Creation stories in Genesis 1 and 2, human beings, including their sexual identities and means of relating sexually, are considered good. The implication is that sexual relating between men and women is edifying, in part, because it is a means for reproduction, necessary for the survival of humans. It is also good because sexuality contributes to holistic human relationships and provides sensual and affectional enrichment.

Humans are not created to be solitary individuals; they are meant to be in relationship with others. The animals, says the text, were not sufficient companions for the original human earth creature. Eve became the most appropriate companion for Adam, as well as the fitting helper and lover. Men and women are to leave their parents and cling to their spouses, becoming one flesh (Gen. 2:24).

From those opening passages on, we find an extraordinary amount of material about sex and sexuality in the biblical text, including both healthy relationships and damaging, destructive ones. While sex and sexuality are not intended to be the Bible's major theme, in the Hebrew Scriptures we find stories about or references to sexual behaviors.

• In Genesis 26:8, there is marital foreplay, with Isaac fondling his wife Rebekah.

• We read about adulterous affairs, not just between wicked people, but also between some of God's chosen ones. We are told of King David's attraction to the bathing Bathsheba, his subsequent seduction of her, her pregnancy, and his plot to have her husband killed in battle so he could not discover David's wickedness (2 Sam. 11:1-27).

• There are rapes, both heterosexual and homosexual, including gang rapes of women, and reference to homosexual rapes of heterosexual men (Gen. 19:1-10; Judg. 19:1-30; 2 Sam. 13:1-20).

• Many men had polygamous marriages. Jacob took two wives (Rachel and Leah). Solomon had 700 wives and 300 concubines (1 Kings 11:1-4).

• Ruth, the godly woman who had a book named after her, was instructed to sneak in at night, crawl under the covers with Boaz, and lie near his loins. Most English translations say near his "feet," but in Hebrew, the reference is further up the legs. The story speaks of Ruth doing so, and then of her eventual marriage to Boaz (Ruth 3:1-15).

• The Song of Songs (Sol.) describes a female lover's breasts as fawns; her body is a mountain of myrrh and a hill of frankincense. A male lover's legs are described as alabaster columns and his body as ivory work encrusted with sapphires.

• There are instructions about coitus interruptus, particularly condemnation of pulling out and spilling one's semen on the ground because, in the case of Onan and Tamar, it broke covenant responsibility to Onan's brother (Gen. 38: 9-10).

• Leviticus 18–20 gives guidelines for not having sex during menstruation, not having sex with animals, not showing one's nakedness, and commentaries on a wide range of other sexual behaviors.

• The Song of Songs 8:3 gives implicit recommendations for foreplay with a woman, including where to place your left arm and what to fondle with your right.

• There was temple prostitution, the religious practice of some who did not follow Yahweh. They had intercourse with a prostitute at the temple for the sake of worship, fertile lands, and financial support of the religious cult (1 Sam. 2:22; 1 Kings 14:23-24; 2 Kings 23:7, 14; Ezek. 8:14).

The Old Testament is loaded with such references to sexual issues. Yet it is also clear that the Hebrews sought to distinguish themselves from their fertility-cult neighbors, whose sexuality was inextricably intertwined with their gods and goddesses. For the most part, the Hebrew people perceived God, not as a sexual being, but as one who stands behind and beyond sexuality. Certainly we find gendered references to God in Hebrew Scriptures, and most of these are male ones, but we also find female images. These male and female images from life tell us some things about God, but God is not fully captured by any of them. Sexuality is a created reality, created by God for the good of humanity.

According to the Old Testament, sex and sexuality—even though not a part of the divine being—are to be celebrated. The most dramatic affirmation of sexuality is in the Song of Songs, where we find pictures of erotic joy between the sexes portrayed as good. The book consists of two lovers, a bride and bridegroom, speaking back and forth to each other. Sometimes the book has been over-spiritualized and understood to be about the relationship between Yahweh and Israel.

There *are* examples in the Hebrew Scriptures of a human sexual relationship being used to describe the relationship between God and humans. Notably, Hosea talks about his marriage to Gomer, a "harlot." This relationship is used as an allegory for God's relationship with Israel: Israel had so often left God behind to worship other gods, but God continues reaching out to Israel and accepting her back. God's faithfulness, fidelity, and forgiveness are shown even in Israel's periods of failure and infidelity.

While this spiritualizing is sometimes appropriate, in the Song of Songs such an interpretation seems to be a misreading of what was intended to be a celebration of love and courtship: "I am my beloved's, and his desire is for me. Come, my

beloved, let us go forth into the fields, and lodge in the villages.
. . . There I will give you my love" (7:10-12b, NRSV).

Proverbs 5:18-19 evokes a similar passion: "Let your fountain be blessed, and rejoice in the wife of your youth, a lovely deer, a graceful doe. May her breasts satisfy you at all times; may you be intoxicated always by her love" (NRSV).

Any faith tradition that includes such poetry among its sacred writings has an appreciation and respect for sex and sexuality. Certainly heterosexual intercourse is intended partly for procreation, as the Hebrew Scriptures make clear. But as we see in such passages, sexual relating is also to be enjoyed as a good gift of God, as powerfully passionate and unifying.

Perhaps because of this unifying power, the Old Testament also makes it clear that sexual relating should take place within particular contexts. It is a special human expression appropriate in some settings and not in others. In Leviticus and Deuteronomy, we find a range of counsel regarding the sexual aspects of marriage, sexual intercourse, adultery, incest, rape, prostitution, male-male sex, and sex with slaves and animals. While we should carefully analyze and critique passages such as those in the Holiness Code (Lev. 17–26), just as we do other injunctions in these sections of Scripture, we should note the text's concern about appropriate relationships.

The Old Testament also makes clear that sexual relating carries with it certain responsibilities and obligations. In some ways, intercourse functions as the marriage bond. In the polygynous and patriarchal culture of the Hebrews, a man who has intercourse with a virgin is obligated to take her as his spouse. Sexual relating has tremendous moral significance. In such sexual uniting, one is making a binding commitment to care for the good of the other.

The New Testament similarly sees goodness, power, and significance in sexuality and sexual relationships.

The New Testament

Between the time the Hebrew Scriptures were recorded and the time the Christian Scriptures were written, Greek philosophy had made a sharp division between the body and the spirit. Although Augustine of Hippo fought this notion in the fourth and fifth centuries after Jesus, he could not fully escape such a dualism in his own theological reflections.

In Greek dualism, which has pervasively influenced the West for the past two millennia, the body is evil, and that makes bodily functions and practices likewise evil. Such a perspective also tends to denigrate women, who are historically more associated with the body, partly because of childbearing and nursing. The spirit, on the other hand, is perceived as the part of us created in God's image. Dualistic perspectives suggest that somehow the spirit needs to be kept separate from the body, this cage which temporarily traps us. The body is perceived as a prison that keeps the more godlike spirit or soul from reaching its goal of union with the divine.

The Hebrew Scriptures had no concept of this division, nor does Jesus, as he is depicted in the New Testament: the person is unified, body and spirit. We are embodied beings, not dismembered ones. The Christian Scriptures more generally fight against this dualism, though the body-spirit split has no doubt influenced some of the New Testament writers. However, the fundamental tenet of Christian faith—that God became *flesh* in the incarnation of Jesus Christ—militates against such dualism.

As in the Old Testament, sex and sexuality were not the primary concerns of Jesus or other New Testament figures or writers. Perhaps under the influence of various early church theologians, too often the church has linked sin primarily with sexuality. Certainly destructive forms of sexual relating can be sinful. According to the biblical record, though, Jesus was far more concerned about the dangers and sins of wealth and the injustices of inequality.

When the rich young man went to Jesus and asked him what

he needed to do to inherit eternal life, Jesus told him to keep the commandments, including injunctions about adultery, truth-telling, respect, killing, and theft. Then Jesus said he lacked one thing: "Go, sell your possessions, and give the money to the poor, and you will have treasure in heaven; then come, follow me" (Matt. 19:21, NRSV).

In Jesus' words, Paul's writings, and elsewhere in the New Testament, when sexual abuses are listed as sins, they are placed alongside equally condemned acts and dispositions such as envy, idolatry, theft, slander, pride, deceit, foolishness, anger, selfishness, murder, and enmity (e.g., Mark 7:21-22; Gal. 5:19-21).

According to the Gospels, the sexual issues Jesus did address are marriage, fornication, adultery, lust, divorce, and remarriage (Matt. 5:27-32, 15:19; 19:3-12; Mark 7:21; 10:2-12; Luke 16:18). In these passages Jesus expanded the notion of adultery and constricted the justification for divorce. Behind such words are the principles of respect, commitment, and care, particularly for women, who could rather easily be used and discarded in Jesus' culture. While Jesus' primary emphasis was not on (narrowly defined) sex and sexuality, he was committed to the formation of deep, meaningful, and intimate relationships.

Many of Jesus' stories, even ones that deal with money or with enemies or with the kingdom of God, have to do with developing relationships of trust and faithfulness. Jesus himself found it essential to surround himself with a group of friends, whom we now call disciples. According to the biblical text, these relationships with men and with women were a fundamental part of who Jesus was.

If we accept the basic Christian understanding that Jesus was fully human as well as fully divine, we also must recognize that he was subject to the same temptations that other humans experience. Unlike painters before them, Renaissance artists frequently depicted the baby Jesus with his genitalia exposed, and occasionally depicted the loincloth-covered adult Jesus in a state of sexual arousal. The apparent point is that Jesus' chastity was real, and his struggles were similar to ours: it would be no great virtue to be chaste if one were not a vigorous sexual being.

It is not unreasonable to speculate that Jesus wondered what a sexual encounter would be like, even though he consciously chose celibacy as a vocation. Novelist Nikos Kazantzakis' movie, *The Last Temptation of Christ*, created an enormous stir in Christian circles. The last temptation, which Jesus ultimately resisted, was for him to abandon his godly mission and settle down with Mary Magdalene, the former prostitute. The film was based largely on Kazantzakis' imagination, but it was not as far-fetched or heretical as some Christians believed. If Jesus was a human being, which the Christian church has affirmed, he no doubt knew what it was like to experience human emotions and passions.

According to the Gospel record, Jesus also did not make marriage the supreme goal for his followers, the only place where God's good will could be best realized. Jesus was most concerned that people would have passion for the reign of God, a passion that would overrule all other desires. He called the disciples to give themselves fully to God's reign. Jesus said, "No one who has left home or wife or brothers or parents or children for the sake of the kingdom of God will fail to receive many times as much in this age and, in the age to come, eternal life" (Luke 18:29-30; and parallels). Spiritual commitment and maturation may happen in the family, but marriage is not essential to such development. The primary social relationship is the disciple group, not the family.

At the same time, Jesus honored marriage and considered it blessed by God. He celebrated with friends at their wedding in Cana, making water into wine as the "first of his miraculous signs" (John 2:1-11). In Matthew 19:4-6 (cf. Mark 10:8-9), Jesus describes marriage with the Genesis term "one flesh." He says, "What God has joined together, let no one separate" (NRSV) or "put asunder" (KJV), language we still hear in wedding ceremonies.

More so than for some of his contemporaries, Jesus viewed marriage as a permanent covenant built on fidelity and nurtured by loyalty, commitment, respect, and love. Such commitment and respect meant guarding oneself against entertaining lustful looks at a person not one's spouse, and thereby being unchaste in heart and thought (Matt. 5:28).

Regarding Paul

Paul spoke most extensively about sexual relationships in 1 Corinthians 5–7. Even more explicitly than Jesus, he counseled single people to remain so, just as he was. Most scholars believe Paul was widowed, so he knew what it was like to be both married and single. In Corinthians, his counsel was based, in part, on his eschatological expectations. He believed that the end of time was near, the world was passing away, and therefore marriage would be a distraction. Marriage would simply make followers of Jesus anxious about the affairs of the world, and Paul wanted them to be concerned about the affairs of the Lord.

Thus Paul affirmed singleness, just as Jesus did by his teaching and example, as a good and right way of living, allowing for more undivided devotion to God. We might want to temper Paul's words with the recognition that his apparent sense of Jesus' imminent return was mistaken. We should note, also, that he makes concessions for those who do not have the gift of singleness. Those who cannot practice "self-control" should marry rather than to be "aflame with passion" (1 Cor. 7:7-9, NRSV).

Nevertheless, we should recognize a distinctive contribution of early Christianity in idealizing permanent vocational celibacy (cf. Matt. 19:12; 1 Cor. 7:7, 32-35). Such a vocation allowed for full commitment to the faith community and a way of breaking out of state-controlled family functions, including the duty to procreate. Intentional virginity especially allowed Christian women direct access to a "higher calling" in the church, eroding the subordination of women to men.

In this same Corinthian passage, which was prompted by accounts Paul had heard about a believer living with his father's wife (1 Cor. 5:1), Paul gave wide-ranging counsel about sexuality. He spoke against incest, sexual perversions, and adultery. He reminded his hearers that "the body is not meant for sexual immorality, but for the Lord, and the Lord for the body" (1 Cor. 6: 13). Because in the act of sexual intercourse, "the two will become one flesh," Paul condemns joining oneself with a prostitute. He indicates that sexual sins are sins against one's own body, which is also a temple of the Holy Spirit. Paul further encourages believers to honor God with their bodies (1 Cor. 6:15-20).

In marriage, Paul urges a *mutual* self-giving of bodies, unless the couple voluntarily chooses—for a time—to abstain so they can be more devoted to prayer (7:3-6).

Unlike Jesus, Paul addresses male homosexual acts on several occasions. In the Corinthian passage where he lists those who will not inherit the kingdom of God, he uses the Greek terms *malakoi* and *arsenokoitai*, sometimes collectively translated as "sexual perverts" (1 Cor. 6:9). Scholars disagree on the specific meanings of the terms, which may carry some reference to same-gender sexual behavior—perhaps pederasty (adult men having sex with young boys) or male prostitution. A similar list identifies some for whom the law is laid down: perverts, adulterers, the unholy and irreligious, slave traders, liars, perjurers, and other ungodly and sinful persons (1 Tim. 1:8-11).

In Romans 1:26-27 and its context, we find Paul's clearest condemnation of homosexual acts, as he understood them. It is also the only biblical passage that deals with sexual relating between women. Paul sees such sexual behavior as "unnatural," saying that "God gave them up in the lusts of their hearts to impurity" (1:24, NRSV). Men who "committed indecent acts with other men," says Paul, "received in themselves the due penalty for their perversion" (1:27).

Willard Krabill more thoroughly addresses homosexuality in chapter 7 of this book. Space does not permit a full exploration of biblical perspectives on this issue here. We should note, however, that several passages in the Hebrew Scriptures also address homosexual acts. The possibility of homosexual rape is mentioned in Genesis 19 and Judges 19, though it is not the focus of those stories. Instead, the "sins of Sodom" are listed elsewhere in the Old Testament as pride, thoughtless ease, abuse of the poor, adultery, lies, and haughtiness (Jer. 23:14; Isa. 13:19; Ezek. 16:49-50). We also must acknowledge the often-overlooked horror of the rape of women implicit or explicit in these passages.

The other biblical places where homosexual acts are condemned are in Leviticus 18:22 and 20:13. This is part of the Holiness Code (Lev. 17–26), which is concerned for ritual purity and being holy to the Lord and separate from the abominations of the Canaanite nations (18:30; 20:26). This code condemns a range of other behaviors such as nakedness, adultery, prostitution, incest, child sacrifice, bearing grudges, wearing "clothing woven of two kinds of material," lying, stealing, and eating sacrifices more than three days old.

The biblical writers had no sense of homosexuality as a psychosexual orientation, a concept that emerged in the late nineteenth century. Those who study the texts should consider the impact of modern notions of sexual orientation—that the basic sexual attraction of some men or women may be to those of the same gender.

In the highly patriarchal Hebrew society, one major concern was that a man might lie with another man "as with a woman." The danger was that male dignity might be offended. From such a perspective, when a man acted sexually like a woman, he degraded himself and lost status—for himself as well as for other males.

In several biblical passages where male-male sexual acts are addressed, they appear to be between unequal partners (adult and child) or in abusive contexts (the Sodom story) rather than in relationships of mutuality, respect, and commitment. Such observations are relevant for interpreting biblical perspectives on same-gender sexual behavior.

Toward Equality

One more word should be said about biblical perspectives on sexuality. Jesus and Paul both sought to break down many of the cultural and religious barriers between men and women. Jesus related to the women around him in a remarkable way. Women were among those who followed him from village to village as he preached and taught, and they were financial supporters of his ministry. He spoke with women openly in public, whether they were potential believers who had come to hear his message, the Samaritan woman at Jacob's well, an unclean (menstruating) woman who touched the hem of his garment, or a woman caught in adultery.

These were not typical male responses in first-century Palestine. Jesus endangered his own standing by relating to such women. He knowingly challenged some of the prescriptions of his religion and culture, and elevated women's status by risking his own.

Too often the Christian tradition has focused on an unequal partnership between women and men, based partly on misunderstandings of biblical texts or on cultural prescriptions. Genesis offers two accounts of God's creation of humans. In the first, we are told that God created humans (generic, not just "man" in the original Hebrew) in God's own image: "So God created humanity in God's own image; . . . male and female God created them" (Gen. 1:27, author's paraphrase).

In the second creation account, which begins in Genesis 2:4b, there is first one human (male), and then the woman is created out of the rib of the man (2:22). The woman, says the text, is created for companionship, so the male human is not alone. She is also created as a "helper suitable for him" (2:18). Sometimes this "helper" status has been interpreted to mean a subordinate role. However, in Hebrew the word for "help" is used elsewhere for the way God cares for God's people. God is the people's "help" (or "helper" or "helpmate"). Together male and female do God's work, just as God is the helper for God's people.

Inequality in the male-female relationship does not occur until after the Fall (Gen. 3). Such inequality, with the male ruling over the female (3:16), is evidence of fallenness, a movement away from God's original intentions. In the biblical story, it is not to be celebrated but lamented.

In the Christian Scriptures, in the writings of Paul and others, we find several passages that address a hierarchical ordering of relationships. Children are to be subject to their parents; slaves must obey their masters; and wives must be subject to their husbands (Eph. 5:21—6: 9; Col. 3:18—4:1; 1 Pet. 2:13—3:7).

In Christian history, early writers did not note that Paul and others did not set up an ideal from scratch but drew on a presumably pre-Christian, culturally prescribed institution (often called *Haustafeln*, "household precepts"). Other-than-Christian writers of the time similarly enjoined women to subordinate themselves to their husbands. Biblical writers who drew on these ethical instructions then modified them with their own Christian teachings.

Paul did not instruct *women* to do anything different, but he did suggest a new pattern for *men:* "Husbands, love your wives, just as Christ loved the church" (Eph. 5:25). Men loving their wives—not wives submitting to their husbands—was the *new* Christian teaching in a culture where love was not part of the cultural expectation for the household.

Paul backed up those words elsewhere with the hope that for

those who have put on Christ, "There is neither Jew nor Greek, slave nor free, male nor female, for you are all one in Christ Jesus" (Gal. 3:28). Such words were revolutionary in Paul's day. Radical egalitarianism is the trajectory toward which Paul and Jesus point us regarding relationships between and respect for men and women.

From the biblical perspective, sexuality is an integral part of our created being, whether we are male or female. It is a dimension of human existence that we honor and celebrate. In terms of genital sexual relating, covenantal heterosexuality is the norm in both the Old and New Testaments. On the biblical line of development, the *quality* of such relationships becomes increasingly important. At their biblical best, genital sexual encounters come within the context of permanent, committed, community-affirmed, monogamous, loving, mutually edifying relationships.

In a broader sense, love, intimacy, and deep personal relationships rooted in Christ are near the heart of the gospel. Persons can embrace such emotions and commitments whether they are single or married. Christians are embodied beings who accept with joy the goodness of their God-given bodies and who respond to such sexual goodness with responsibility, sensitivity, and care.

Discussion Questions

1. Do you think the Christian church has made progress in moving from what some critics call a "sex-negative" attitude in recent years?
2. Are gender-free references to God important to you? Why or why not?
3. Can you think of examples of how the Greek concept of a division between body and spirit continues to affect us today?
4. Why do many Christians seem to think sexual sins are

more important than sins of greed and wealth?

5. How does Jesus' attitude toward women impact us today? How should it?

6. How do you respond to the idea that a true understanding of the biblical text does not support a hierarchical relationship between males and females?

3

The Gift and Intimacy

Willard S. Krabill

WHEN WE THINK about *intimacy*, we often reflect society's corruption of the term and society's preoccupation with sexual matters. We equate "being intimate" with sexual intercourse, and in so doing, we empty intimacy of its deepest meaning. They are not synonymous. We must recognize that the common societal use of *intimate* and *intimacy* is a counterfeit of what we, especially Christians, should mean by true intimacy. Sexual intercourse is only one small, nonessential part of true intimacy in a world that acts as if it is the only thing.

Intimacy and love also are not the same. Intimacy is a dimension of love. I can love the people of my neighborhood, but I am not intimate with all the people in my neighborhood. I need personal relationships to meet my human needs. Humans of all ages need to be loved, to be understood, to be accepted, and to be cared about. We need to be taken seriously, to have our thoughts and feelings respected and held in confidence, and to be trusted.

These statements describe our human need for loving, intimate relationships, not the need for sexual intercourse. We are made for relationships: relationships with God through Jesus Christ, relationships with each other, and relationships with ourselves. The most energizing relationships are intimate relationships. Intimacy is not only desirable; it is also a real need for everyone at every age.

As a physician, I have shared in the deepest moments of people's lives, the good and the bad: birth, first illness, accidents, marriages, addictions, rejections, reunions, and deaths. Never have I seen anyone die from the lack of sexual intercourse. I have, however, seen many people die premature deaths because they feel rejected and lonely, and they lack intimacy. They don't know that they are cared about and prized by another person and that they matter to another person. To achieve the worthwhile goal of becoming intimate with those we love, we need to know what it is and is not, what creates it, and the barriers and aids to developing intimacy.

What Is Intimacy?

Webster says intimacy is sharing what is intrinsic and essential. Other sources define it as *familiarity*, *friendship*, or *privacy*. A church leader, Harold Bauman, defined intimacy as "the experience of a close sustained familiarity with another's inner life; it is to know another person from the inside."

Rod Cooper says, "The word *intimacy* literally means *into-me-see*. Intimacy is the ability to experience an open, supportive, compassionate relationship with another person without fear of condemnation or loss of one's identity. It is knowing another person deeply and appreciating them anyway."

Once, while assisting a heart surgeon with an open-heart operation, I was asked to put my finger inside the beating heart to break up a calcified heart valve. The surgeon said, "That's getting pretty intimate with a person, isn't it?" In a physical sense, he was right. But that intimacy is nothing compared to the experience of communicating on a deep level with a person who is awake, sharing, and communicating in a setting where I, like that heart patient, am vulnerable and also taking risks.

Some years ago, wide attention was focused on intimacy because of a poll taken by Ann Landers among readers of her newspaper column. She asked women to respond to this question: "Would you be content to be held close and be treated tenderly and forget about the 'act,' sexual intercourse? Answer yes or no and give your age." Over 100,000 readers responded, and 72 percent replied yes: I would be content to be held close and be treated tenderly and forget about the act. Forty percent of the respondents were under forty years of age. Here are some of the replies:

• From Columbus, Ohio: "I am under forty and would be delighted to settle for tender words and warm caresses. The rest of it is a bore and can be exhausting. I am sure the sex act was designed strictly for the pleasure of males."

• From Anchorage, Alaska: "I am twenty-six years old, to be exact. I want three children, so obviously I need more than conversation. After I have my family, I would happily settle for separate rooms. Sex doesn't do a thing for me."

• From Kansas City: "I am fifty-five and vote yes. The best part is the cuddling and caressing and the tender words that come with caring. My first husband used to rape me about five times a week. If a stranger had treated me like that, I would have had him arrested."

• From Texarkana, Texas: "Yes, without the tender embrace, the act is animalistic. For years I hated sex and felt used. I was relieved when my husband died. My present mate is on heart pills that have made him impotent. It is like heaven just to be held and cuddled."

Obviously, there were many "no" answers as well (28 percent), but the nature and tremendous numbers of the "yes" answers give evidence of a serious problem in male-female communication in our society. The Associated Press quoted Landers on the poll: "The importance of the sex act is overrated. Women want affection. They want to feel valued. Apparently having sex alone (in and of itself) doesn't give them the feeling they are valued."

"As for men," she added, "too many are using sex as a physical release, and it has no more emotional significance than a sneeze. There is a tremendous lack of communication. It is troublesome" (1985).

When Ann Landers later asked her male readers the same

question, the overwhelming response was no: I would *not* settle for being held tenderly and forget about the act. Only 8 percent said yes, and almost all of those men were over sixty years old.

The following response from New York represents the essence of many: "After a year of marriage, my wife said, 'Let's just cuddle.' The following day, I suggested that we go to her favorite restaurant. When we got there, I told her we weren't going to be seated. Instead, we would just stand by the kitchen and smell the food. (We are both forty.)"

From Brisbane, Australia: "Anyone who would settle for being held tenderly is looking for nothing but companionship. I suggest he buy a dog" (1995).

Clearly, differences in male and female biology, psychology, and conditioning help explain the differences in the above responses. However, sexual apathy is common in North America among both sexes, especially among women. During the sexual revolution, a kind of "sexual anorexia" developed in our society.

With increased promiscuity and emphasis on sexual technique, commitment became almost irrelevant for many. The chief aim was to try every kind of sexual expression possible and not be uptight in doing so. Instead of this being a utopian experience, however, a certain anxiety developed. People were asking questions, such as "How am I performing?" and "Why am I sleeping with this person I hardly know and don't even like that well?" In spite of much sexual activity, people felt empty. People sought counseling and wondered why all their "lovemaking" was so unsatisfying. In that situation, sexual anorexia set in.

In my medical practice, the most common sexual complaint I have heard over the years, by far, is from the woman who has lost her sexual interest (which she had initially). She says, "I just feel like a thing. He just uses me, I feel like a thing." I have heard it over and over again. These persons need intimacy. We all need intimacy, a relationship closer than the physical.

I think that usually my female patients were lacking intimacy in their marriages because it was never there in the first place. The common North American cultural dating practices and style do not foster the development of genuine intimacy. The absence of intimacy is not surprising when the dating scene is characterized by such terms as "making out" and "scoring," with friends asking, "How far did you go?" In many relationships between unmarried people today, the question is not whether intercourse will be a part of it, but when. Making sexual intercourse the objective is destructive to true intimacy.

Dating in North America takes place in a milieu that encourages experiencing physical intimacy before developing the other dimensions of intimacy. Emotional, aesthetic, spiritual, and intellectual intimacy should precede physical intimacy. It is emotionally disastrous for a person to attempt physical intimacy before her or his personal identity is even established (as in the case of a teenager).

Intimacy is the unending marvel of understanding and being understood by another person. If people want true intimacy, their relationships must include certain characteristics.

What Creates Intimacy?

The first ingredient and step in building an intimate relationship is *friendship*. Are you drawn to the person—not the person's body, but the person? Do you really like her or him? Can you imagine spending hours with that person, talking about things that are really important to you? Can you imagine going to that person's home and spending time together in the context of his or her family? Can you imagine being that person's close friend and not letting "that sex thing" get in the way of your friendship? Some of the greatest intimacies in the world are between people who for one reason or another are not dating, engaged, or married, nor do they intend to be married. Friendship is the first ingredient of intimacy.

Another part of intimacy is *acceptance.* Do you accept the person for who he or she is as a person, not as a body or sex partner? Or do you think you may need to fine-tune the other person a bit, make a few changes here and there, or manipulate her or his personality to fit better? In an intimate relationship, both people need to be accepted. If we are assured of acceptance, we do not need to defend our failures. We know we are not on trial with an intimate friend. An intimate friend sends a clear and unconditional message, "You are okay, worthwhile, and valuable." Those who experience the unconditional love of God are best able to love and accept other people unconditionally.

Communication is absolutely essential for developing an intimate relationship. This must be open, honest communication—no deceit or pretending, no lies, and no hidden agenda. Intimacy requires open people who are willing to bare their souls. Closed people cannot achieve it. Openness is frequently a problem for males. Deep sharing involves vulnerability, and vulnerability does not fit the usual stereotype of the macho image that some men try to portray. But we must share deeply if we are to become intimate with the ones we love.

Lillian Rubin, in *Intimate Strangers,* suggests that in our society, conditioned as men are, they are often denied effective emotional expression. For some young men, sexual intercourse becomes the main way emotional content can be expressed. This explains why genital expression is such an urgent matter for so many men. It is conditioned learning and thus can be unlearned.

Some women do not honestly communicate their feelings and their values, and continue compromising their demands for intimacy. As a result, they will make poor choices—poor choices of friends, men who do not understand intimacy, men who fake intimacy to get their way, or men who are so badly conditioned regarding male-female relationships that they simply do not know *how* to be tender, sensitive, honest, and vulnerable.

Equality is another important ingredient of intimacy. To dominate another person destroys intimacy. The worth of both partners in a relationship has to be equal. There can be no coercion, no power play, no manipulation, and no using the other for selfish purposes. Equal! Whether the intimate friends are of the same sex or differing genders, both must express and experience total equality. I must feel just as important to you as you are to me. Today male dominance and the double standard are not acceptable and should be over. In an intimate relationship, both persons must come from an equal power base.

Trust is an ingredient of intimacy that is an overlooked essential in many relationships. To become intimate with someone is risky. There are many emotional risks in deeply sharing and caring, and that is scary. Why? Because we are afraid we might be rejected. Few if any experiences are as devastating as being rejected. Developing trust is so important and critical. If we do not send honest messages, if we pretend to be trustworthy, a painful outcome is inevitable. If we want to become intimate, we have to become very vulnerable.

Dependability, loyalty, and honesty all build the trust that we need before we are willing to risk sharing our deepest feelings. Deceit and dishonesty are quite prevalent in our society. Trust is in short supply, as revealed in the world of soap operas and the 50-percent divorce rate. Before we can risk disclosing ourselves, we need to be able to trust. Trust allows us to put our fears and our deepest feelings in our friend's hands, knowing that they will be treated carefully. No reasonable person communicates what is deeply personal in an environment infected with doubt, uncertainty, failed expectations, social betrayals, slighted feelings, or confidential sharing exposed. Few things bind us to each other like a promise kept. Nothing divides us like a promise broken.

The greatest intimacy is possible between people who have *shared values*—those who share the same lifestyle and life goals. True intimacy is unlikely to develop if two people are on a different life quest, a different road or journey, and have a different worldview. In an intimate relationship, shared values make all the ingredients of intimacy more attainable. When people have a shared faith in Jesus Christ and a shared faith community, these add a dimension to an intimate relationship that our secular society does not comprehend.

Jesus illustrates God's intention for each of us to experience intimacy. He was renewed by his visits to Bethany. John 12:1-3 tells about Jesus' visit to the safe house of Mary, Martha, and Lazarus, where he went to enjoy deep friendship, to rest, and to be renewed and encouraged in his prophetic mission.

Affection is an ingredient of intimacy. Do you have feelings of affection for the other person? Does your face light up when his or her name is mentioned? Do you really care when the other person is hurting? Do you desire to be close to each other, and do you feel encouraged in each other's presence?

Touch is another important ingredient of intimacy—affirming touch and not exploiting touch. Intimate touching makes us feel better, not guilty. If the touching makes us feel important and not used, then it is an affirming touch. Until and unless we know the difference between affirming touch and the exploiting touch for inappropriate sexual arousal, we cannot trust. If we cannot trust, we cannot achieve intimacy.

True intimacy means being with another person in a way that is closer than the contact of two bodies (that, incidentally, is no big accomplishment). It is the interaction of those persons in a relationship of knowing and trusting that is closer than just the physical. When physical intimacy is divorced from true intimacy, it is hollow and meaningless. It leaves one frustrated and often breaks up the relationship. Sexual intercourse never creates intimacy. Sexual intercourse can energize and cap the relationship only when all the other components are already present.

To develop true intimacy takes lots of *time*. It is a process, a dynamic, growing experience. There is no instant, easy way to experience true intimacy, despite what the soap operas, movies, and songs may tell us. It takes time to develop true intimacy and to be fully available to other persons, to share their joys and hear their suffering. True intimacy cannot be fallen into and out of in rapid succession. Two people need long stretches of time for them to develop all the characteristics of true intimacy.

It is not realistic to talk about developing intimate relationships with many people. We have time for only a few really intimate relationships. We should select them well and build them strongly and solidly.

Commitment is the final ingredient and step. We make a decision to really be there for the other person. This is the promise we intend to keep. True intimacy is more than friendship, equality, or communication. It requires commitment, the kind of loving commitment that keeps us present for and involved with the friend, partner, or whomever, and keeps us caring and loving over time. Such intimacy keeps two people together, not just when the road is smooth and maybe sensuous, but also when the road is rough and sweaty.

Many nongenital friendships are far more intimate than many marriages. The commitment might be between two dating partners who commit themselves to saving the genital relationship for marriage, and that too is a commitment that builds intimacy.

To become the genital partner of another human being is to become very vulnerable. The trust that should be present for sexual intercourse to take place can hardly occur outside of commitment. Sexual intercourse is the most self-giving, self-exposing exchange two people can make. It is precisely because it is so self-giving and self-exposing that the act of rape is so devastating, violent, and inexcusable.

Two old lines have fooled many people: "Prove your love"

and "You would if you loved me." The real proof of love is the demonstration that our commitment and intimacy are so strong, so solid, and so faithful that we can remain with each other and be true and faithful to each other without getting involved in genital intercourse until marriage. That is true love—proof that I want you and not just your body. Without true intimacy, genital activity is often distancing and not uniting.

Today the mechanical stimulation of genital nerve endings often passes for getting intimate, but that does not satisfy our need for intimacy. Some truly intimate friendships do lead into marriage and a fulfilling sexual relationship. When they do, that is great, but only after the other dimensions of intimacy are achieved. The marriage of two people who have already experienced true intimacy is one most likely to endure. Their physical intimacy is most celebrative because the other ingredients of true intimacy are present.

Unfortunately, I have had to work with many married couples who have never experienced real intimacy in their lives, some who are hardly friends. They just got entangled in physical infatuation and were never intimate.

And now *love*. Love is bigger than intimacy. If we think in New Testament terms, it is much bigger.

As we understand and experience intimacy, then we can begin to understand love. When we are able to say, "I love you," to someone with whom we are intimate, love takes on its true meaning—not the meaning expressed in popular songs, television, and movies, but the deep Jesus-difference meaning. When people who are intimate say, "I love you," they are saying, "For you, I would give all of myself."

Barriers to Developing True Intimacy

The barriers to developing intimate relationships are the opposite of the ingredients or requisites of intimacy. If trust is a requisite, the lack of trust is a barrier. There are, however, some particular barriers that deserve special mention. Two barriers to intimacy will be discussed here.

First, many people use sexual intercourse to shield themselves from the scariness of true intimacy: from the exposure, the unmasking, and the vulnerability. Many individuals use sexual promiscuity to avoid real intimacy. Others use sexual athletics to bolster self-esteem, to combat anxiety, or to avoid genuine communication. Constantly searching for sexual thrills without truly sharing each other's personal worlds tears the physical aspect of sex from its integrated place in the whole person. A meaningful and fulfilling relationship needs more than sexual intercourse to sustain it.

Coitus, we must recognize, is the only aspect of intimacy that some people experience. When this is true, even this dimension will end in disillusionment. We may overburden intercourse with our real need for emotional, verbal, and spiritual intimacy; for the expression of all kinds of feelings; for overcoming loneliness; for finding fulfillment in life; and for feeling needed and wanted. If we do so, we ask far more of intercourse than it can possibly deliver.

A second barrier is rigidly held traditional masculine and feminine roles, and socialization to maintain stereotypes. The more readily people accept and live out traditional male and female roles, the less likely it is for them to develop intimate relationships.

To promote the development of intimacy, we must help our children and help each other achieve the goal of being fully human, not just of being a typical man or typical woman. Children can be reared to combine the so-called feminine attributes of gentleness and sensitivity with the so-called masculine attributes of strength, independence, and confidence. In the process, they recognize that they are all human attributes and of equal value.

It is high time we learned what Carol Gilligan has taught us in her book *In a Different Voice*. She says that women perceive the moral problem as one of relationships, care, and responsibility. Their perception is just as needed and valid as men's perception of the moral problem as one of rights, rules, and justice. The ethic of justice proceeds from a premise of equality, that everyone should be treated the same. The ethic of care rests on the premise of nonviolence, that no one should be hurt. The typical moral premises of men and women are equally needed if we are really to understand human relationships in any setting.

We have noted what intimacy is and what it is not, what creates intimacy, and the barriers to developing intimate relationships. We have known for a long time that the most important and protective factor against emotional and physical illness is the presence of an intimate and confiding relationship, one of trust, in which feelings can be shared whether or not sexual intimacy occurs.

As we consider the strength and power of intimacy, we need to heal the most pervasive and damaging rupture in the human family, the rupture between the sexes. The foundation for more intimate relations between men and women is being laid today in many places and in many ways. Progress is being made, and there is much hope. The borders of the shared worlds of men and women are being enlarged, but there is a long way to go.

Aids to Developing True Intimacy

Sex education is a part of that growth toward true intimacy. But sex education needs to be sexuality education. It needs to be intimacy education. Too much sex education still deals largely with how babies are made, diseases to be avoided, or how to produce orgasms. Acquiring loving habits and attitudes and acquiring the capacity for true intimacy requires more than a study of the technology of arousal. It requires, first and foremost, the understanding that genital relationships are not even required for the experience of intimacy. Single celibate people can fulfill all of the criteria for experiencing true intimacy.

For many of us, a Christian worldview is an essential, enabling, and invigorating aspect, providing promise for the future. This Christian worldview values the renewal of Christian family life, the development of true human intimacy, and the nurturing of mature faith in a church community. Such a worldview can help us resist the pressures of our consumer society and focus on what matters most in life—love for God and for each other.

We all need to experience intimacy at all stages of our lives. In the discovery of true intimacy, we have the possibility for a new era in male-female relationships, in family relationships, in all human relationships, and in the possibility for world peace. Developing truly intimate relationships is a worthwhile goal for all people.

Discussion Questions

1. Can the ability to be tender, sensitive, honest, and vulnerable be taught and learned? How?
2. How does having shared values make all the ingredients of intimacy more attainable?
3. What convinces us that it is safe to risk disclosing our innermost thoughts and selves to another person?
4. A couple is married thirty-plus years, and the husband declares he is no longer committed to this relationship. What is wrong with this picture? How would you counsel the couple?
5. What steps might be taken to heal the rupture between the sexes?
6. Some men have difficulty expressing their emotions. Can they be helped to do this better? How?

4

The Gift and Young People

Michael A. Carrera and Anne Krabill Hershberger

Adolescent Sexuality: Looking Above the Waist*

For the majority of parents, school policy makers, and government officials, the phrases "family life," "sex education," and "human sexuality" are simply code words for school programs discussing sex acts, contraception, and safer sex techniques. Many believe that these words camouflage instructions on who does what to whom, in what position, how many times, and how to avoid undesirable outcomes while "doing it." In many communities, sexuality education has come to mean explanations of below-the-waist genital acts. Therefore, the primary challenge for those working in sexuality with teens is to communicate a holistic, above-the-waist definition of sexuality and sexual expression.

While issues of genital-sexual behaviors and their potential outcomes are critical to explore with young people, an obsession about adolescent intercourse continues to dominate our work. These efforts have created an overwhelmingly genital focus and an all-around unhealthy environment for discussing sexuality with young people. We wrongly portray sexuality as an event. What a profound disservice this is to teens because it narrows and distorts their understanding of themselves. In the meantime, we continue to reduce sexuality education to discussions about disease, life-and-death issues, and a burdened and compromised future. By arousing their fear, we engage in a pro-

---

* In this section, Carrera's chapter "Adolescent Sexuality: Looking Above the Waist," in *Lessons for Lifeguards: Working with Teens When the Topic Is Hope* (1996), is reprinted with the author's permission.

cess to terrify them about sexuality and its many expressions.

Adolescent sexuality is not an activity; it is not an event; it is not a behavior. Instead, adolescent sexuality is an extensive, complex, and potentially joyful area of life. It is spiritual, intellectual, emotional, religious, and cultural, as well as biological. Discussions of "sexual activity" should not merely include intercourse and contraception. Adolescent sexual activity includes kissing, flirting, touching, holding, hugging, fantasy, sensuality, and erotic behaviors.

By spending so much time in schools and community agencies on relentless discussions about genital sexual behaviors, and by saturating teens with videos about abstinence, safer sex, and contraception—we have in effect performed a "sexectomy" on our young people. We have separated sex from the rest of life. We have divided and compartmentalized the genitals from the whole person. We have reduced an essential and fulfilling life force by describing it *in genitalia* only, which we then deny.

I believe that we need to stop looking below the waist. I believe we need to raise our sights and look to the full person. This task represents the principal challenge in the sexuality field today. I believe that raising our sights will signify a quantum leap from a narrow focus on sex acts, behaviors, and genitals to a more holistic, organic view of sexuality and sexual expression.

Of course, such a leap will be difficult, since many of the influences that shape sexuality (Hollywood, the media, television) relay messages that are superficial, cosmetic, and slick. These powerful factors reinforce the genital focus that we have all been taught to believe constitutes our essential sexual nature.

A holistic grasp of sexuality redefines it as an essential life force, both organic and inherent to the total person. The holistic philosophy maintains that sexuality is expressed in a variety of ways, not singularly through our genitals alone, whether by ourselves or with a partner.

Sexuality is expressed through our social, gender, and family roles. It is expressed through nongenital means of affection, love, and intimacy. It is expressed erotically, sensually, and yes, genitally. However, genital sexual expression is only one fiber of the total fabric, and one fiber does not constitute the whole cloth. Many, many fibers woven together in unique patterns constitute the whole cloth that is a person's sexuality.

Thus through lectures, discussion groups, and videos, we must emphasize that genital-sexual behavior is only one aspect of sexuality, and that there is a great capacity for varied sexual expression. If we must obsess, let it be about body image, gender roles, social and family roles, sensuousness, and the vast ways of showing affection, love, and intimacy. These fundamental elements constitute the whole person; they are the woven fibers creating each person's sexual potential.

Our sexuality lessons must explore above-the-waist issues like the impact and role of gender. Many young people are excited by opportunities to gain genuine insight into this complex dimension. However, society tends to eroticize all relationships between men and women and to objectify and depersonalize the gendered aspects of the individual. These elements continue to influence teens, who are very interested in trying to discern what it means to be male and what it means to be female.

Socialization remains strongly gender-specific and, at times, limiting. Strong social factors create segregated male psyches and female psyches, which can make our work challenging, to say the least. For these reasons, gender-role exploration should constitute a major part of all sexuality education.

Another dimension of adolescent sexuality that needs our attention is body image, or how young people feel about and perceive themselves, and how they perceive others. Confidence and feelings of security about the "rightness" of one's body can facilitate healthy expressions of sexuality. Conversely, doubt and anxiety about one's body can inhibit healthy sexual expression.

For example, adolescent males have received the message, loudly and clearly, that they should do and not feel. Their masculinity rests on a strong body that is able to perform. Adolescent females learn that "looks count." All of their biological changes during puberty are monitored and interpreted through a filter of the ideal cultural appearance. Young women quickly learn to view their bodies cosmetically and superficially; they are socialized to use these standards and look to others for validation of their femininity.

An adolescent concept of self is greatly influenced and powerfully affected by gender socialization; by lessons in closeness, caring, and tenderness toward people of both sexes; and by values within a familial and societal context. Only recently have we begun to pay attention to the struggle of males and females of all ages to control their deepest feelings lest they be labeled "inappropriate" to their sex.

If we want future generations of adults to interact with others in secure, intimate, and loving ways, then the sexual learning of adolescents must include an exploration of feelings, affection, and intimacy in the context of gender expectations and in the context of simply being a human being.

Life Options—Hope

The author of the previous section, Dr. Michael A. Carrera, has developed one of the most successful models of adolescent pregnancy prevention and health promotion programs in the United States. He began it in New York City's Harlem area more than ten years ago, and it has now been replicated in eighteen other communities. People refer to it as a "life options" model. The components of the program include the following:

1. A broadly defined family-life and sex-education program that includes both parents and their teenage children.

2. Medical and health services, from primary care by physicians and nurses to counseling in family planning (which emphasizes abstinence while providing contraceptives to teens who are already sexually active).

3. Mental health services (professional social workers and counseling).

4. Efforts to improve participants' academic performance, including academic assessments and help with their homework.

5. A program designed to build self-esteem through performing arts.

6. An individual sports component based on the premise that various sports activities—from tennis and swimming to basketball and the martial arts—encourage the development of self-discipline, the mastery of skills, and the control of impulses.

7. A career-awareness training program and Job Club conducted by employment specialists who provide participants with the concrete skills needed to gain employment (Corning and Noyes: 23-25).

Corning and Noyes summarized the experiences of this and other programs that have had some success in meeting the needs of youth. They found that the three top risk factors for adolescents, regardless of setting or economic status, were substance abuse, violence, and risky sexual behavior. They also found that successful programs differed from less-successful ones in that they incorporated multiple methods, environments, and participants. One-dimensional programs were not as effective.

When used in combination, consistently successful program components were the following:

1. Life-skills development and practice.

2. Interactive, experiential teaching methods that stress normative beliefs (NO, everyone is NOT doing it; YES, good conduct will be rewarded) and that provide basic, accurate infor-

mation about consequences.

3. Family involvement in positive ways.

4. Active mentoring and leadership by peers, with strong adult sponsorship and management.

5. Access to health services and referral/linkages to other community resources.

6. Attention to media influences on behavior and media reinforcement of positive messages.

7. Economic and educational incentives and/or employment opportunities.

When young people have dreams and goals but see no way of reaching them, those dreams quickly fade. To meet their need for acceptance and belonging, they easily succumb to peer pressure. For too many teens, that peer pressure leads to substance abuse, violence, and risky sexual behavior. Multifaceted programs have met some degree of success in preventing young people from becoming involved in these negative behaviors.

These programs call for adult participation and leadership at many levels and in many areas. Adults with special interest and/or expertise in business, counseling, health care, the arts, athletics, and education, among others, have a significant and needed contribution to make to young people. As the successful programs show, it is important for these varied persons to collaborate and coordinate their efforts for effective results.

Young people are best served when the caring adults who interact with them and who serve as their leaders, mentors, and advocates are committed Christians who base their own lives on Christian principles.

1. These Christians will believe in the *worth* of every young person—the cooperative and well-disciplined, the troublemaker, the shy and fearful, and the loud-mouthed. They will care for the physically attractive, those plagued with acne, the exhibitors of fashion extremes, and the slovenly. They will value the intellectually bright, the not-so-bright, and all those in between. They will delight in the athletes and the physically

compromised—all of whom are experiencing newly discovered sexual appetites.

2. Christian leaders will believe in the *potential* of every young person. They will rejoice with those who have had endless opportunities to develop many interests and skills. They will encourage those whose every interest has been thwarted by lack of finances, discouragement, and poor educational resources. They will show God's love to those who lack personal support and have no one in their lives who cares what becomes of them.

3. Christian mentors will recognize the crucial importance of *positive interpersonal relationships* in every young person's life. They will therefore strive to connect each youth with wholesome peers and create opportunities to interact with Christian adult role models in their areas of interest. They will serve as coaches in the development of social skills and graces that foster good relationships and lovingly guide youth in changing some negative behaviors. They will communicate that the young person is missed when he or she does not appear. They will discuss matters of sexuality in a knowledgeable, caring, and open manner.

4. Caring Christian adults will introduce young people to the most reliable anchor for their lives—*Jesus Christ* and his unconditional love, acceptance, forgiveness, and promise never to abandon them.

If young people have contact with such adults, that can make the difference in whether they have hope or despair, experience joy or suffering, set goals or give up, feel self-worth or self-hatred, contribute to the well-being of their peers or isolate themselves; and find eternal salvation and peace or be lost.

Exposure to a wide variety of caring adults can be helpful for young people. Yet a recent poll conducted by the National Campaign to Prevent Teen Pregnancy validates the fact that teenagers want to hear from their parents about sex, love, and relationships. Parents have far-greater influence on their children's sexual decision making than they might think. The National Campaign released ten practical, research-based tips for parents to help their children avoid teen pregnancy. Here they are in abbreviated and adapted form:

1. *Be clear about your own sexual values and attitudes.* Communicating with your children about sex, love, and relationships is often more successful when you are certain in your own mind about these issues.

2. *Talk with your children early and often about sex, and be specific!* Initiate the conversation; and make sure it is a dialogue, not a monologue.

3. *Supervise and monitor your children.* Establish rules, curfews, and standards of expected behavior, preferably through an open process of family discussion.

4. *Know your children's friends and their families.* Welcome your children's friends into your home and talk to them openly.

5. *Discourage early, frequent, and steady dating.* Group activities among young people are fine, but allowing teens to begin steady, one-with-one dating much before age sixteen can lead to trouble.

6. *Take a strong stand against your daughter dating a boy significantly older than she is. Do not allow your son to develop an intense relationship with a girl much younger than he is, or a woman much older.* The power difference between younger and older can lead your teenager into risky situations.

7. *Help your teenagers to have options for the future that are more attractive than early pregnancy and parenthood.* Help them set meaningful goals for the future, talk to them about what it takes to make future plans come true, and help them reach their goals.

8. *Let your children know that you value education highly.* School failure is often the first sign of trouble.

9. *Be media literate—know what your children are listening to, watching, and reading.* You can always turn the TV off,

cancel subscriptions, and place certain movies off limits. You cannot fully control what your children see and hear, but you can certainly make your views known.

10. *Build a strong, close relationship with your children from an early age, but remember, it is never too late to improve a relationship with a child or teenager.* The first nine tips work best when this is in place. Express love and affection clearly and often, listen carefully to what your children say, spend time with your children engaged in activities that they like, be supportive and interested in what interests them, and help them build self-esteem (Campaign Update: 4).

This chapter does not cover everything young people need to experience their sexuality in the best way. It does, however, indicate some areas that deserve attention if young people are to develop the most wholesome sexual attitudes and behaviors. Well-planned interventions by caring Christian people can counter the powerfully seductive and often harmful but attractive sexual messages bombarding young people in the culture at large.

Discussion Questions

1. What is needed to help young people reach their dreams and goals and thereby avoid the problems many youth experience?
2. How might young people who seem to have no goals or ambitions be helped?
3. What combination of services for young people might congregations develop? How could their success or failure be measured and shared?

5

The Gift and Singleness

From Human Sexuality in the Christian Life*

OUR THINKING about the sexuality of singles quickly centers on the meaning of words. The term *single person* can apply to a person of any age.

Many Kinds of Singleness

Single is a label that takes in the graduate student who has every intention of marrying later, the engaged couple, the widow and the widower, along with the career single. The divorced person, who may either be grieving or relieved, is also single. The term applies to those who would like to be married and to uncoupled homosexual persons, as well as to those individuals who define their singleness as part of their devotion to God.

Indeed, all these people are legally single. Different experiences and attitudes result from their varied reasons for being single. The complexity of the single experience becomes clear when we contrast singleness as a lifestyle with marriage. The married person works at the task of building intimacy with another person by establishing financial, legal, housing, familial, and physical ties. The single person tends to spread these ties around.

Emotional ties with other people can be deep, intimate, and of long duration; but the public vow to be there in the future

---

* Portions of the chapter on "Singleness," in *Human Sexuality in the Christian Life* (1985) are reprinted here with slight editing and permission from the Mennonite Church and the General Conference Mennonite Church.

for the other is not offered. In other words, the single person chooses to work at intimacy without making use of all the social structures available.

Most societies have assumed, however, that the married life is the only reasonable way to live as an adult human being. In some societies, marriage is a matter of survival. Powerful mating rituals and customs exist in all groups. In our culture, advertising links food, jewelry, and hygienic products with kisses and declarations of love; it thus supports the equating of health and love with marriage. The feasting and material wealth showered upon a couple at a wedding powerfully bestows the community's blessing with clarity that most single people never experience.

Yet, in spite of the powerful incentives to marry, some people in every culture and generation remain single. In older societies, these single persons often lived with and contributed to the extended family system. In North America, this practice has almost disappeared as both the nuclear family and singles have asserted their right to be independent of the claims and gifts of the family clan.

Entry and Reentry into Singleness

The breakdown of the extended family system has broadened the number of opportunities for people to find family, trust, and intimacy in relationships that are not biologically based. For the single, however, this situation carries with it both the promise of a life rich in good relationships with all sorts of people and the danger that this new family will not form and the individual will be left emotionally barren and financially vulnerable.

Therefore, to find one's place in a community of persons apart from one's family, a series of sexual-emotional tasks must be accomplished. The nature of these tasks depends upon the age of the single person.

For singles in their teens, the task is to build an identity clearly enough to allow them to reach beyond the family with some degree of security. Teenage singles must increasingly show themselves willing and able to leave home. Growing sexual awareness adds a prod to this process of becoming independent.

Most young adult singles have left home and chosen a vocation, but the process of setting up a community of friends is still in the making. This community of persons both grows and diminishes when the single person moves, when friends get married, and when married friends start having children. As the changes keep happening, the urge for a long-term commitment of some kind may grow stronger. Many people get married during this period.

For singles in their late twenties and early thirties, the question of long-term commitments may become more pressing. Many women begin to be aware of the biological urge to have children. A singleness that had previously been experienced as a good thing begins to be less acceptable. The demands and frustrating claims of one's vocation may begin to make body tiredness more noticeable. The desire to be held, comforted, and touched is felt more frequently.

People who have been married but are once again single are sizable groups in our communities. The Scripture was always sensitive to this group, giving special directions to the community to see to the needs of the widows. Those who are widowed may receive more sympathy than divorcées, and yet they have much in common: family life, friendship networks, finances, and emotional stability are dramatically altered. The sexual issues involve reestablishing and again identifying how one is a sexual person when the genital relationship is gone, making peace with loneliness, finding the graces of solitude, and learning to reach out again to strengthen or rebuild trust in one's friends.

Asserting Control

The role of the single person in the larger community is uncertain. Especially in the younger years, it is not clear what place the single person is going to assume, what the nature of the person's long-term commitments are, and what can be expected from him or her in the future. Older singles, as well, often need to make clear over and over to the people in their community their intentions toward others. Divorced or widowed people soon discover with some astonishment the many and varied ways married people express insecurity around single people. For example, some females who are once again single occasionally report detecting body language of married women that communicates their discomfort when single women talk with their husbands.

Although married people, too, must face issues of self-control and mutual consent, for them the basis for sexual decision making is clearer: "What will enhance our relationship?" The wedding ritual clarifies the couple's place in the social scheme. The community has given permission, made room for the new couple, and expects sexual intercourse to take place. Once this ceremony has taken place, the larger community trusts the couple to live responsibly with each other and in relation to others.

Because the position of single persons is not clear, they are vulnerable to the larger community's power to exert control and impose punishment when they do not meet interpersonal behavioral expectations. Sooner or later, the single person must determine whether to assume responsibility for managing her or his own sexuality. This managing will entail decisions about such things as the nature of personal relationships with people of the other and the same gender, whether married or single; decisions about developing a family-like support group, especially if living away from one's biological family members; decisions about sexual expression, appropriate touching, and physical intimacy; and decisions about one's entertainment choices.

If the single persons do not manage their sexuality responsibly, the community will try to do so for them, rightly or wrongly. Sooner or later, the larger community will have to admit its uncertain feelings toward single persons in its midst. Hopefully, single people can help to educate and influence the larger community on behaviors and attitudes that foster positive relationships with single people.

Single Life Honored

People in Bible times lived in a world of couples. Marriage defined "the good life." Yet Jesus honored the single state while upholding the sanctity of the marriage bond. Though he cast no shadow on matrimony, he saw in life things more important than meeting sexual needs and building families.

Although Jesus saw in marriage a divine design for persons, he was aware that marriage might obstruct the will of God (Luke 14:20). Some may have the gift to live a life of singleness for the sake of the kingdom of God (Matt. 19:12).

Vocation for Paul

Paul also regarded marriage as a valid option for Christians (1 Cor. 7:36). But it is commonly felt that he thought of celibacy (voluntary singleness) as the ideal state. This view grows out of several statements made by Paul in 1 Corinthians 7.

The seventh chapter begins with a startling statement: "It is good for a man not to touch a woman" (7:1, KJV). This may be Paul's statement, but many scholars think he is quoting from the letter the Corinthian church has sent to him, and then replying to that letter.

In any case, he did choose a celibate life for himself for at least part of his life (Paul may have been a widower), and he wishes the gift of celibacy for everyone (7:7). He accepts with approval those who also choose the celibate life instead of marriage (7:37-38, 40).

In Pauline tradition, marriage is clearly *not* seen as a sin or a lower state of being. In Ephesians 5, the marriage relationship is used to depict the intimacy between the church and Jesus Christ. But in the Corinthian letter, Paul is dealing with marriage, not as an ideal form, but as a way of life that has practical effects on the lives of people. He suggests that marriage is good for those with strong sexual drives (1 Cor. 7:9). He knows that marriage and undivided loyalty to Christ will often be in tension (7:33-35).

Paul does not equate marriage with sexual freedom, for he envisions periods when the couple may abstain from sexual intercourse for the sake of prayer (7:3-5). This can imply that marital intercourse and religious devotion do not go together, but it may only be a realistic recognition that attention cannot be given fully to both at the same time.

Great New Creation

Paul's clear sense of vocation, of his life having a purpose, shaped his thinking about singleness. For him, God's work did not end with the first creation. It continued as God in Christ shaped a greater gift: a new heaven and a new earth. The Christian is one who in faith takes part with God in making the new kingdom. Anyone who wants to work with God (who is creating this new world) or who even wants to be a citizen in this new world, has to let go of some of the values of the old order. Since this age is passing away, all its institutions, including marriage, have no permanent value (1 Cor. 7:29-31). In the new era, marriage will not have a place.

The kingdom of God has broken into history with the coming of Christ. Marriage is no longer merely an order of creation or a duty to give birth to succeeding generations to keep the covenant alive. The "holy seed" has come in, and through this new peoplehood, God's purposes in the world are being realized (Isa. 6:13). God has lifted from marriage the pressure to provide children for the survival of the covenant community. No longer do believers need to see childlessness as the absence of God's favor (1 Cor. 7:8; Matt. 19:12).

Living as though the new realm were already fully here, however, requires an inner freedom, a faith that God's work will continue into the future, and a sure belief that this kingdom is possible and real. As Paul put it, "Those who have wives should live as if they had none" (1 Cor. 7:29).

When Paul recognized the urgency of the times, he saw how awareness that "the world in its present form is passing away" (7:31) could lead to a life less complicated by many loyalties, commitments, and involvements. The single person could be more free to be a co-creator with God in a more focused and active way. In Paul's mind, single people with the future in view are needed in the church because "the time is short" (7:29).

However, if marriage is now not a general obligation, neither is singleness. In 1 Corinthians 7, Paul shows both the married state and singleness as a leaning: "To be married is to lean to the pull of the old world which is passing away but which has not lost its reality; to be unmarried is to incline toward the tug of the eschaton's freedom" (Cartlidge: 322-323). This statement almost equates singleness with heaven, but Paul himself was careful not to make singleness more godly than marriage or to make celibacy a necessity for the Christian.

Paul appears to have thought of marriage and singleness as the context out of which a person offers service to God and experiences relationship with God. In 1 Corinthians 7:17, 20, and 24, all the verbs imply that the individual has an active role in determining the daily details, the specific quality of one's days.

Biblical Concerns

Attractive as the ideal of celibacy may seem when viewed through the eyes of Paul and the experiences of those who have modeled it, many single persons do not feel called to that way of life. A single person may desire a sexual relationship with another person or may already be involved in one. What counsel can the church give to such a person?

What follows are two sets of questions that single persons and their friends, families, and pastors may find helpful in discerning direction. These inquiries intend to lead toward a Christian course of action by testing the results of the various choices offered to single persons. This testing, we believe, will lead toward a clearer understanding of the biblical principles that the church has always supported.

Testing One's Personal Condition

The first set of questions deals with the history and condition of the individual:

1. What would or does a sexual relationship mean in the whole context of this person's life and in this relationship? What is the nature of the relationship being considered: a passing one or a really deep one? What is the meaning of a sexual relationship for this person now? Does the person want a sexual awakening? Is he or she seeking intimacy or trying to bolster femininity or masculinity? Will the sexual relationship be a product of anxiety? Will the couple share the love and caring that they feel for each other?

2. On the other hand, what would be the purpose and function of self-denial at this point? What would be its goal?

3. Finally, what is this person's experience of God at the moment? The answer will reveal a good deal about this person's reality (adapted from Goergen: 185).

Consequences of Sexual Intercourse

The second set of questions touches more directly and clearly on the motive and the consequences of intercourse at this juncture for the couple. These are questions they need to ask each other and themselves:

1. Do we understand the physical and emotional aspects of

sexual arousal? Do we know anything about each other's health? What will be the consequences for our health?

2. Does this behavior fit with our life plans? Does it help us reach our goals?

3. Does this behavior fit with who I am? Am I making the decision to do this, or am I yielding to pressure?

4. What message are we conveying by this activity? Do we both understand the message? What is the motive behind my message?

5. Are we coming at this decision from equal power bases? Is there any degree of coercion, pressure, unfair persuasion, or subtle bribery? Is either of us using power to influence the decision?

6. Is the decision based on present realities or on fantasy?

7. Does it strengthen the structures that are important to us? What kind of social institutions are created by this behavior: a home, a family, a welfare agency, or none? Does it strengthen and stabilize, not just immediate personal relationships, but the social framework as well? How will relationships with our families be affected? Does it contribute positively to the movement of which we are or want to be a part?

8. Have we heard God's Word, gone to the Scriptures, sought the Spirit, and prayed about it together?

9. What is the personal spiritual impact of our sexual behavior? Can I continue to experience God's leading and presence?

10. What now is our decision?

Like Couples Engaged

The above questions ought also to be asked of the couple who is engaged. These persons, while still unmarried, remain in the same uncertain relation to the larger community as they were when they were uncommitted. Many of their commitments and bonds have not yet been made public. Although the two may know each other well enough to decide to marry, much remains unknown.

Even when both persons are fully united and fully committed, neither exerting unequal pressure on the other, their decisions do have implications beyond themselves. No two people can so isolate themselves from family or friends that their decision will have no meaning for the group of which they are a part. This seems especially true for those of us with a strong sense of family, church, or congregation with whom sharing is the very essence of our being.

Sexual Harmony

The above is a caution. The engaged couple, however, has many important positive sexual and emotional tasks to accomplish during the engagement. One task is to establish good communication and trust patterns around the whole subject of sex. Sharing freely keeps one from nursing unrealistic expectations of the other. It strengthens each one's willingness to do whatever will help the other to be comfortable and experience pleasure. It will help each to gain control over the fears and uncomfortable feelings that he or she brings to marriage.

For sexual harmony to exist in a marriage,

> each partner must accept the other as the final authority on his or her own feelings. . . . They are telling each other that they acknowledge and accept without question the fact that they are individuals, separate but not separated, different but not dissimilar, and that their happiness must flow both from the delight they find in their differences and the security they derive from their similarities. (Masters and Johnson: 48)

A second task for engaged couples is to share, appreciate, and delight in differences. Our culture does not teach us to do this well. When two people fear differences and use their differences to define themselves sexually, they tend to hide or deny or make excuses for their feelings. The engaged couple can do much to insure the happiness of their marriage if they learn from the beginning not to flee when it becomes clear that there is a difference in sexual values and body responses.

Choosing a Style

Getting to know the real differences in one's partner will give a person occasion to reflect upon, accept, or reject the sexual heritage of his or her parental home. Families have a sexual style. Some families touch each other a lot; others touch each other only on certain occasions. Part of the delight of an intimate relationship is realizing all that one took for granted in childhood.

A third emotional and sexual task is setting the ground rules for the degree of openness to others that the persons want their relationship to have. A good barometer for discovering this is to ask, With whom will it be all right to share sexual problems and pleasures? Family? Trusted friends? A counselor? Our pastor? To state early on to seek community resources and feedback can be one of the building blocks to a secure marriage.

Affirming Singleness

In treating the sexuality of singleness as we have, we are assuming several things:

1. We are assuming that the biblical limitation of sexual intercourse to marriage is a condition meant to guide people to well-being and wholeness. Even when we are aware that some biblical comments appear to be influenced by the cultural and religious beliefs of the times, we affirm that the overall influence of the Scriptures is toward harmony, intimacy, wholeness, and well-being. Prohibitions and cautions about certain forms of sexual activity should be seen in the light of the positive goals of wholeness, health, and justice toward which the Scrip-

tures want to lead us.

2. The special contribution of the New Testament to our thinking on singleness is that it clearly gives single people a place in the community and a purpose and vocation. Therefore, we are assuming that sexual wholeness and fulfillment cannot be found without communication with other people and commitment to them.

> Lasting sexual fulfillment cannot be found apart from, nor can sex be substituted for, action directed toward meeting one's need to know God, one's need for community, or one's need for a meaningful vocation. Possibly this suggests a reason why there is such a preoccupation with sex in our culture. Failing to know God, failing to find real community, and failing to realize a calling through satisfying work, people are desperately trying to fill the vacuum with sex. (White)

3. We assume, too, and strongly affirm that periods of singleness, whether at the beginning, middle, or end of life, can be fulfilling periods of life.

Discussion Questions

1. Currently in U.S. culture approximately 40 percent of the adult population is single at any one time. What are the advantages and disadvantages of living life as a single person?

2. What can each of the following do most effectively to incorporate single people into the community? The single person? Married persons? Congregations?

3. When people live alone, they are responsible for all the activities of daily living, such as housekeeping, car and house maintenance, finances, taxes, and social activities. What might ease these burdens?

6

The Gift and Marriage

Willard S. Krabill

WE COME into the world as single people, albeit extremely dependent upon other people for our survival and development. As noted in the previous chapter, persons who are single beyond this initial dependent stage can experience affection, have intimate friendships, and have a whole life of fulfillment. Marriage, however, continues to be a choice for the majority of people in most societies for part of their adult lives. Singleness and marriage should be equally valued.

The term *marriage* has held different meanings for people in other times and places as well as among people currently. These include the ideas of being "married" in spirit but not legally; co-habitation; common-law marriage; arranged marriage, through a choice not made by the pair; civil ceremony; and a ceremony of religious commitment. In each situation, it is assumed that the couple is identified as a social unit separate from others at least in living arrangements. It is also generally assumed that sexual intercourse is a part of the couple's relationship.

In this chapter, *marriage* will refer to the lifelong commitment sealed through vows made by the partners to each other, witnessed by others, and legally sanctioned.

Many in today's general society do not regard a marriage license as a prerequisite for them to meet their needs for a more or less "permanent" relationship, personal identity, companionship, economic support, sexual intercourse, or bearing children. So why get married? What does the relationship of marriage and sexuality mean for Christian people?

Why Get Married?

"Marriage provides a sense of emotional and psychological security . . . and opportunities to share feelings, experiences, and ideas with someone with whom one forms a special attachment. Desires for companionship and intimacy are thus central goals in contemporary marriages" (Rathus et al.: 412). Today, in general society, access to sexual intercourse is less likely to be a motive for marriage because more people than earlier believe that premarital sex is acceptable between two people who feel affectionate toward each other.

Marriage does, however, legitimize and restrict sexual intercourse. This allows the couple to assume that any children the woman bears also belong to her spouse. Marriage provides an institution in which children can be supported and socialized into adopting the norms of the family and its culture. It permits the orderly transmission of wealth from one family and generation to another (Rathus et al.: 411).

When marriage vows are taken seriously, they really do mean something and are not conditional. "For better or for worse" are powerful words. They imply that the commitment made will endure when the road gets rough and sweaty instead of smooth and sensual, when job loss occurs, when the money runs out, and when a diving accident renders one a twenty-eight-year-old paraplegic. This kind of commitment surely reflects true love and fosters a sense of security.

Marriage allows people to have the freedom to be themselves and to express feelings without the fear of losing the relationship. This freedom to be open and honest builds trust that is so crucial in forming an intimate relationship.

The public aspect of marriage—a wedding or civil ceremony—helps us define who we are in our couple relationship and in our relationship to the community. The community perceives us as a legal social unit and bestows certain expectations upon us. We expect that publicly made commitments will lead one to pause before breaking them.

By comparing marriage with the alternative of cohabitation, we may gain some insight for answering the question, "Why get married?"

Cohabitation

Some cohabitants never intend to get married, but many other cohabitants consider this arrangement a trial marriage. Two people cohabiting may claim commitment to each other. But until it is validated publicly in the presence of witnesses to whom the couple is accountable, there is something tentative about the commitment. If it is tentative, it is not a total commitment. Either one has made a commitment or one has not. If we say, "Let's try it and see if it works," we provide an escape and remove the incentive to make it work. Marriage cannot be practiced beforehand.

In *The Living Together Trap*, the author says that although most women enter the arrangement expecting a monogamous relationship, many find their partners cheating on them. They further discover that the men had a prior pattern of living-together ventures about which the women had not been told (Rosen). This data is not reassuring in an age of widespread sexually transmitted diseases like AIDS, herpes, chlamydia, and hepatitis B.

Approximately 40 percent of cohabiting couples eventually marry. The casualty rate for those marriages greatly exceeds the rate for those who had not lived together prior to marriage. One study conducted over twenty-three years found that couples who cohabited before their marriage increased their likelihood of divorce by 50 percent when compared with those who did not cohabit before marriage. Those couples who had cohabited also indicated a lower level of marital satisfaction generally (Axinn and Thornton). Those who are leery of commitment are more apt to stray after marriage as well.

As in so many male-female relationships, the women are

more vulnerable. Unequal expectations of the relationship are common. Studies show that women, more frequently than men, enter the relationship expecting permanence. Too often, one or the other is secretly saying, "I'm afraid my love for you won't last, so I want an escape hatch just in case." When sexual intercourse has been involved, a breakup brings suffering especially for the woman who, more often than the man, expected this kind of a relationship to last. The data simply is not there to support the notion that cohabitation results in better marriages, less abuse, less violence, fewer affairs, or a less-painful breakup.

Thus far in the discussion, we have considered marriage and cohabitation as living patterns involving people in general. What does our biblically based understanding of marriage and sexual intercourse mean for Christian people?

Christian Understanding of Marriage and Sexual Intercourse

Study of the New Testament reveals affirmation of monogamy and marriage and only negative statements about either adultery or *fornication*, the (KJV) word used to describe unchastity or illicit sex of all kinds, including intercourse outside of marriage. Marriage is affirmed in the New Testament, and sexual intercourse is placed firmly within the context of marriage. But among Christians in North American culture today, an increasing number are staying single, delaying marriage, but still engaging in sexual intercourse. Is the biblical stance on this issue obsolete for people in today's culture?

When deciding whether or not to engage in sexual intercourse before marriage, there are things to consider in addition to the biblical admonition. In this chapter we highlight fourteen reasons for abstinence from my perspective as a Christian physician with a background of many years in family practice, obstetrical-gynecological practice, and college health practice.

They emerge from my personal experience and observations. I have had a great deal more than average exposure to the sexual experiences of a wide variety of people, many of whom have been young women, young married couples, and college students.

Reasons to Abstain from Premarital Sex

Premarital sex tends to diminish personal happiness and predisposes the participants to sexual boredom.

People are "doing it more, but enjoying it less." Many have guilt and anxiety about it. People who believe "What does the Bible say?" is a relevant and important question will feel especially guilty. It is my observation that those engaging in sexual intercourse outside of marriage are not happier and are not having greater sexual pleasure. Premarital sexual affairs frequently complicate a relationship and lead to painful splitting up.

One's first or early sexual intercourse experiences always carry much meaning. Psychiatrists, regardless of their personal value systems, repeatedly comment that one's initial sexual experience constitutes a significant emotional passage or event in one's life. A couple's relationship is somehow different after sexual intercourse has been a part of it.

The notion that sexual intercourse is casual inevitably lessens its impact, its importance, and its potential for ecstasy. To reduce a life-uniting experience to one of "just another physiological function" is perhaps the greatest of all indictments of premarital sex.

Premarital sex is often not the result of a mutual decision.

For something as "heavy" as sex outside of marriage, as far-reaching in its consequences, as complex in its meanings, as full of potential for pain as well as joy—for this just to "happen" is really immoral and irresponsible. So much should be considered, so much should be shared, and so honest must be the communication that it cannot be "right" when the couple is just "carried away by passion." In premarital sex, a sufficient dialogue and process of decision making has usually not occurred.

Premarital sex usually "takes over" the relationship.

It tends to become *the focus,* and the couple spends less time and effort on getting to know each other as total persons. In one school year, for example, two sexually active college women came to me at the health center to say they had stopped using the pill. They were no longer engaging in coital activity with their boyfriends. Each couple had decided that because their sexual activity had come to dominate their relationship, they would discontinue it. They wanted their doctor to know about this change.

Each person should ask, "Do I want the one I am engaged to or dating to be interested in me because of who I am—the real me—or just because of how I perform in bed?" When the growth of physical intimacies precedes the growth of shared interests, beliefs, intellectual intimacy, emotional intimacy, aesthetic intimacy, and spiritual intimacy—then the relationship becomes distorted, and the physical relationship tends to dominate. There are already far too many marriages, as well as single relationships, where there is sex without true intimacy.

Premarital sex confuses and complicates communication between two people.

People are created for relationship. Singles—male and female—can have meaningful relationships with many people of both sexes. Sexual intercourse is one special kind of relationship between people. To be in relationship requires communication, so *honest communication* becomes all-important in considering when, where, and with whom one will have a sexual relationship.

Until the permanence of the commitment is sealed, coitus

tends to make one unsure of the message and the motive of one's partner. What is the motive: self-gratification, satisfaction of physical urges, or consideration for the partner's long-term best interests? What message is being sent?

Premarital sexual relationships break up far more couples than they strengthen.

Personal observation, backed by the results of studies, shows that when sexual intercourse enters the premarital relationship, the odds that the couple will split are increased. Many people cannot handle it. Often a female adolescent gives a classic statement: "When I gave in, he lost interest." At a sexuality seminar on our campus, a discussion question was posed: "What do you say to the person the next morning in the dining hall line?" It is sad to see the frequency with which a couple that might have developed a long-term partnership breaks up after premarital sex begins.

Premarital sex denies one the opportunity for the most meaningful sexual experience of all.

We look forward to knowing that two people are coming together in full sexual union after saving that special gift—that portion of their being—for the occasion of final commitment and celebration. That will not be possible for those who engage in premarital sex.

People will be shortchanged if they arrive at the celebration of marriage, of sacred promise, and have nothing special left to share by way of physical union. For all young people, we covet an experience of being able to achieve unity of spirit, mind, purpose, and the promise of life together, and to seal it at marriage as a unique expression of physical unity with a sexual expression not previously shared. That is special!

The uniqueness of human sexual intercourse can best be realized within a permanent, exclusive relationship of complete trust and security. If this potential for ecstasy is misused, one is cheated. The sexual expression that could do so much to seal and enhance a marriage tends to become more of a physical exercise than a celebration of true love, commitment, promise, and trust.

Premarital sex impairs one's sense of community.

As noted in chapter 5, one's decision about sex outside of marriage is not really a "do your own thing" issue. When it is perceived that way, both the relationship and the community is shortchanged.

Great experiences are made greater when we can publicly share them. We all have a human need for celebration. Sexual intercourse can be a wonderful milestone in life. When this life-uniting experience begins, people desire and need the shared joy, affirmation, celebration, and support that goes with Christian marriage. To ask that this new relationship be secret and unannounced diminishes and stresses the relationship (Smedes: 146).

Sexuality involves all of life: emotional, mental, social, spiritual, and physical.

Premarital intercourse infers that our sexual urges are physical "needs" which must not be denied. We speak of having "raging passions." We say, "We can't be blamed if they just take over, you know." We are not created that way. No one should fall for that line. Scientists even question whether the human has a sexual instinct in the way animals do. We have sexual appetites and urges, but the satisfaction of them is not essential to physical or emotional health.

In medical practice, we often hear statements like these: "My husband needs it." "My boyfriend has to get it somewhere." *Desires* it? Yes. *Has* to have it? No. People (male or female) survive and are healthy without experiencing sexual intercourse. One of the secrets of a positive and mature life is the experience of being able to forego or postpone something.

This is one of the secrets of happiness for anyone, married or single, living a fulfilled life in spite of many unfulfilled desires.

Premarital sex is unfair to the physical relationship.

Premarital sex tends to be detrimental to the realization of full physical enjoyment. It often occurs in settings "where no one will find out" and is often done with guilt and in a hurried manner. This frequently produces tension. With tension comes less relaxation, less confidence, and less enjoyment. With tension and anxiety, the male may experience premature ejaculation, and the female may have discomfort and frustration.

Premarital sex may predispose one to sexual dysfunction. It frequently is detrimental to the eventual achievement of the best physical sexual adjustment. One hears people claim that premarital sex enhances early sexual adjustments within marriage. Such statements are increasingly being questioned in the medical and psychological professions.

Performance pressure often sneaks into premarital sexual relationships, and it may carry over into many marital relationships. Couples may think that they have not "made it" unless they do it "right" or achieve orgasm. This kind of pressure can be detrimental to the relationship.

Premarital sex contradicts what human history tells us.

It is presumptuous to suppose that we know better than millennia of human experience, mediated through our Judeo-Christian heritage. This cumulative experience has demonstrated that it is best to reserve sexual intercourse for covenanted marriage. Premarital sex did occur in past centuries, but the recommended sexual codes have persisted. Would our sexual codes have endured so long if they were not valid? Human experience speaks loudly.

Premarital sex tends to produce spiritual anxiety, thus risking God's disfavor.

The Scriptures do not view fornication with acceptance or favor. There has been controversy over the meaning of the word *fornication* in the Bible. Does it apply to engaged couples having sex, or does it refer only to promiscuity and other forms of illicit sex? But the whole tenor of the Scriptures, the high status assigned to marriage, and the condemnation of adultery—all affirm a sex-within-marriage position.

New Testament scholar and professor Howard Charles writes in his paper "Sexuality in the New Testament" that in the New Testament, "coitus is set firmly in the context of marriage. . . . Nowhere in the New Testament is there a formal discussion of what constitutes the real nature or essence of marriage." However, Charles goes on to conclude that

> the conception of marriage to which we are led by these materials has a foundation covenant which is consummated by coitus and which inaugurates an interpersonal relationship between a man and a woman having the potential of embracing all areas of their lives. Both Jesus and Paul intend marriage to be permanent and regard fidelity in coitus as obligatory on both husband and wife. It is in the context of a permanent contractual or covenantal relationship involving an ongoing shared life between a man and a woman that coitus is to have its place both expressing and implementing the marriage union. (11)

Detailing what the Bible says about premarital sexual union is not the focus of this chapter. In chapters 5 and 6 of *Sex for Christians*, Lewis Smedes expresses well the viewpoint reached through my personal Bible reading and experience.

Premarital sex detracts from the meaning of marriage.

A decline in the stature of marriage is evident in society and also in the church. Extramarital sex contributes to the tentativeness of marriage and the *trial marriage* kind of thinking. The meaning of marriage suffers when persons have sexual intercourse while engaged, while living together unmarried, or outside a marriage. The finality and the irreversibility of the marriage commitment constitute its significance and its potential value, giving it strength and enriching the sexual expression and message.

I asked a patient whose marriage was floundering and near breakup, "Are you having sexual intercourse with your husband?" "No," she said, "there's nothing for it to say anymore." It is the message, not the physical sensation, that is uniquely human about our sexuality.

Premarital sex is costly.

People do get hurt: what was created by God for our pleasure often becomes our pain. Today many say sexual intercourse outside of marriage is okay as long as no one gets hurt. Who is so wise that he or she can predict who will get hurt? Which motorcyclists, riding without helmets, are going to have their heads smashed? Which in a group that uses alcohol will be the one out of ten who ends up addicted and alcoholic? When people decide to experiment with sexual intercourse outside of marriage, which ones are going to be hurt? The hurt may only be perceived in the future, and no one can accurately predict it.

Another frequent observation from my medical practice is that, for those who had sexual intercourse before marriage, the frequency and intensity of intercourse sharply diminished after the ceremony. Might this have a relationship to the earlier-mentioned research findings that living together prior to marriage increases the likelihood of eventual divorce?

Premarital sex risks pregnancy and sexually transmitted diseases (STDs).

One might have expected a physician to present this reason

first, but thirteen other important reasons were given before these obvious ones.

In the literature about prevention and treatment of STDs, one rarely reads about the only reliable method of prevention: having only one sexual partner through fidelity within marriage and abstinence outside of marriage. If each person would confine her or his sexual activity to one partner, the STD epidemic could be terminated. This is not likely to happen soon. Hence, we need to recognize the tremendous toll experienced by individuals and society as the epidemic of STDs, which now includes AIDS, continues to grow.

The United States' National Center for Health Statistics reported in the *New York Times* (Oct. 5, 1996) that for the first time in nearly two decades, the rate of births among single women declined in 1995; and for the fourth year in a row, the teenage birthrate dropped. This indeed is good news. We need more study to discover why this is happening. Some of the data do reveal that sexual activity among teenagers has waned. There is also evidence of increased use of longer-lasting birth control methods. Yet the number of births to singles is still too high.

When children are born to an immature parent or parents, the negative results are well-known: mothers often drop out of high school, live in poverty, and experience unproductive lives. Children more frequently are born prematurely, have low birth weight, and suffer poor health. They have greater incidence of abuse, neglect, and learning difficulties. They more often are raised by only one parent. Chapter 11 will include more on this.

We can assume that people who engage in premarital sexual intercourse do not expect to acquire STDs or become pregnant. Yet many do not use condoms to help prevent STDs, and additional birth control methods to prevent pregnancy. Many adolescents do not use contraceptives because of their personal attitudes toward sex outside of marriage. They often have the illusion that STDs or pregnancy "can't happen to me," or they think that sexual intercourse must be by impulse and that to prepare for it is wrong.

As many married couples will testify, no contraceptive method is foolproof. Sexual intercourse outside of marriage is particularly immoral if those who engage in it are not ready to accept responsibility for the consequences, including pregnancy. Since a great many persons in extramarital relationships are not ready for pregnancy, that is still a valid reason for abstinence.

In Support of Covenantal Marriage

These fourteen reasons reveal my personal position regarding premarital sexual intercourse. They all have meaning for me, but not all may have meaning for others. I believe our sexuality is a good and beautiful God-given dimension of our being and our personality. It is a serious matter to misuse sex for selfish purposes, out of bounds, or in any nonmutual or exploitative way. In 1 Corinthians 6:18, Paul says, "Flee from sexual immorality."

I do not believe, however, that sexual sins are unforgivable or unique. I believe that the sins of the flesh (carnal nature) are not limited to sex acts; lying, jealousy, and cheating are equally serious. I believe that sexual sins are not sins because they are sexual but because they are hurtful. I have seen beautiful examples of forgiveness and starting over in those who have been guilty of sexual sins.

I believe one can start over in one's sexual practice and lifestyle. Where there are wounds, not all the scars are erased and not all the memories are eradicated. One can, however, become a virginal person (male or female) in God's sight once again.

I urge that sexual intercourse always be a mutually decided event. For premarital sexual intercourse to just "happen" is especially sad. When unmarried persons decide to become sexually active—and some will—they should be responsible enough to use a birth control method. I will continue to be a friend, confidant, and professional advisor to those persons. But when I am asked for my opinion, I must share as I have here. I believe that premarital sex is not the best way to go. We will be happier and closer to God's will for our lives if we keep sexual intercourse within the marriage covenant relationship.

It is rewarding to note how following biblical guidelines serves our best interests. Covenantal marriage is the most satisfying. Abstinence before marriage and monogamy within it would eliminate worry about unwanted pregnancies outside of marriage, STDs, most HIV infections (AIDS), and the emotional pain that derives from multiple sexual partnerships. Why do we ignore the guidelines? They work. They really do.

We must challenge persons who choose marriage *not* to take their cues from general society's attitudes toward permanent relationships or the marital example of many public figures. Instead, better cues are available from the teachings of Jesus, from those who take their Christian commitment seriously, from the wisdom of those who have experienced the trials and rewards of long-term marriage, and from the examples of those who after forty, fifty, sixty, or seventy years remain loving and faithful till death parts them.

Of course, there will be conflict, but couples can experience the reward of resolving conflict. The ability to work things out is remarkably improved when walking out is not an option. When we can walk away from conflict, we do not grow.

Think of two mature, fully committed Christian people exchanging their marriage vows, surrounded by a supportive community of people who love them and share their faith and values. They are in an ideal situation to nourish and sustain their marriage commitment. Avoiding commitment is the prevailing ethos in the society at large. It is not easy to form solid bonds and maintain one's vows in an environment where relationships frequently fall apart.

"Christians must begin to live joyfully and faithfully in their marriages—right in the midst of today's marital chaos. . . . Our society desperately needs marriages built on a biblical foundation that combines freedom and sacrifice" (Sider and Sider: 38).

Marriages are special blessings for the church. In turn, the church can bless and strengthen the commitment. Christian marriage also affords a spiritual intimacy—a shared faith, a shared worldview, and a shared sense of God's leading and presence. All these foster a depth of intimacy that is difficult for non-Christians to comprehend. When the church family can celebrate and support the union, another level of extended family is added to support the commitment and to empower the couple as a new home is established.

Within this new union, commitment to God is paramount, and commitment to each other has been blessed by the faith community. Thus the gift of sexuality can flourish and be expressed in a myriad loving ways. Within a monogamous, committed, covenant relationship *not* preceded by premarital experimentation, the marriage partners will be able to be themselves and learn to make love together. They will not be on trial with each other, will not be compared with previous partners, will not feel they have to perform, and will have the freedom to experiment endlessly. They can say no as well as yes, laugh at themselves, and love each other unconditionally. Chapter 9 will say more about *keeping* excitement and romance alive in marriage.

Marriage is an excellent choice for those who are ready and able to make a lifelong commitment. After that commitment has been made, the meaning of sexual union is multiplied and made celebratory and joyous to a greater extent than otherwise possible. The supporting Christian community wants to and is in a good position to affirm its members' engagements and celebrate their marriages.

Discussion Questions

1. What is it about a premarital cohabitation relationship

that increases the odds of divorce by 50 percent if that
couple eventually marries?

2. What is observed in marriages that discourage some
   young people from entering that kind of relationship?
3. Why does premarital sexual intercourse often complicate
   and confuse communication in a couple's relationship?
4. What do you think is essential to safeguard a marriage?

7

The Gift and
Same-Sex Orientation

Willard S. Krabill

HOMOSEXUALITY. Apart from abortion, there are few words
that elicit a more emotional response or that are more divisive
and polarizing than this word. This is true in communities
large and small, in Congress, and especially in Christian faith
communities. Nearly all Christian communities are wrestling
with this issue, especially regarding the acceptability of gay
marriage. In *The Good Book,* Peter Gomes observes that this
issue has become so central to right conduct and belief that any
compromise is considered capitulation to error (145).

On this area of sexuality, one can justifiably ask, "What
more is there to say?" So much has already been said and written about homosexuality. The polarization emerges from differing interpretations of biblical texts, the "unnaturalness"
(for the large majority of people) of same-sex attraction, and a
rather pervasive discomfort and insecurity that people have,
not only about discussing sexual matters, but also about their
own sexuality.

Frequently, people who are "different" seem threatening to
others. Gomes states, "More than any other social or theological issue of our day, this one engages us at our most fundamental level of existence and raises disturbing questions about
our own sense of identity, of morality, and of the nature of set-
tled truth" (144). I have read many books and unpublished pa-
pers by writers on all sides of the issues in this chapter. Equally sincere interpreters use the same biblical texts and draw con-

tradictory conclusions.

It is conceivable that when and if the twenty-first century turns into the twenty-second (perhaps sooner), the contents of a chapter on this topic would be quite different. In other words, our understanding of this topic is incomplete. As we live, study, do further research, pray, and discern in our faith communities, we hope new insights will clarify our understanding, give us all more-loving attitudes, and decrease or eliminate the polarization present today. As with any controversial topic, it is wise to keep an open and inquiring mind when considering it.

This chapter is not intended to be a complete or final study of homosexuality. Its purpose is not to prescribe a position on the issue of gay marriage, for example, but to suggest that we keep the issue in perspective. We should not let homosexuality dominate our study of sexuality or be a litmus test of one's orthodoxy.

This chapter will not repeat the broader examination of homosexuality found in *Human Sexuality in the Christian Life* (chap. 2, sect. 7:104-120). We recommend that readers study it.

Chapter 2 (above) provides a discussion of relevant scriptural passages. For the purposes of this chapter, we will identify some definitions and contexts, areas of general consensus, and areas of continuing disagreement. These will be followed by a personal response to the issue, some observations, and identification of future tasks for Christians regarding the homosexuality issue. This chapter does not prescribe a particular position. It is an appeal for an attitude or stance that allows Christians to remain in fellowship and loving dialogue even while disagreeing on an issue like homosexuality.

Definitions and Context

It is important that we discuss homosexuality in the context of our overall sexuality. As noted earlier, we are sexual throughout life, regardless of our life's situation. In the Genesis story, sexuality was not added to the human design *after* sin occurred. We are whole creatures—body, mind, and spirit. These whole beings are (in God's good wisdom) sexual beings. We do not *have* bodies; we *are* our bodies, just as we *are* mind and spirit.

Jesus came to us in a body—a physical, sexual, male body. If we believe that as God's Son on earth, he was fully human, we must accept that he had to deal with male-female interaction as we do. When he spoke of the attraction of one sex for the other, as in Matthew 5:27-28, he no doubt knew about this from personal experience. It is reasonable and scriptural to assume that Jesus experienced sexual attraction and had erections and wet dreams. Hebrews 4:15 says he was "tempted in every way, just as we are—yet was without sin."

Any discussion of homosexuality today must note the variety of identities and terms currently used. We must do this if we wish to recognize the importance of these variations as real to those generally marginalized by the dominant culture. In this chapter we use the terms *homosexual, gay,* and *same-sex oriented* interchangeably, not intending to favor one term, even though many in the gay community do prefer a term for various reasons.

The term *lesbian* refers to a female same-sex oriented person. I will use *homosexual* or *gay* to refer to either or both the male and female same-sex attracted person. A *bisexual* person is erotically attracted to (or has more than usual identification with) members of both sexes.

This chapter cannot deal with all the variations in sexual affinity and behaviors. For instance, those who consider themselves transgendered often cross the usual (for most of us) boundaries of the expected gender roles for men and women. They have a more fluid sense of traditional male or female identity. Since homosexuality is a major issue dividing society and the church, our focus in this chapter will be limited to that variation.

Homosexuality is defined from a variety of perspectives: psychological, biological, sociological, medical, and political. I served on the study committee that developed the study guide mentioned above, *Human Sexuality in the Christian Life*. We defined *homosexuality* as the emotional, erotic, and physical attraction toward people of one's own gender. Note that the word *attraction*, not the word *behavior*, is used in this definition. Homosexual people, just like heterosexuals, may or may not act on those feelings of erotic attraction: they may be celibate or may be sexually active.

Much confusion occurs in the church and elsewhere when we use the term *homosexuality* and do not clearly say whether we are referring to an orientation and attraction *or* to certain behavior, meaning genital activity. It is often assumed that anyone calling for Christian charity toward homosexual persons is thereby condoning promiscuous, cruising lifestyles. This assumption is both inaccurate and unfair.

There *are* some who incorrectly define the word *homosexual* to mean same-sex genital activity. This denies the reality of same-sex orientation apart from genital activity and unfairly makes the term *celibate homosexual* into nonsense.

When homosexuals and homosexuality are discussed in church conference settings, it is apparent to me that the various participants do not have the same images in mind. One person assumes that all homosexuals frequent gay bars and bathhouses and are sexually promiscuous. Another thinks of the friend, son, or daughter who is a committed Christian, reads the Bible, prays, teaches Sunday school, claims salvation through Jesus Christ, and is knocking on the door of the church and asking, "May I come in too?" Or, "Can I remain in the church?"

The single word *homosexual* or *homosexuality* cannot be used to capture both of these images; misunderstandings will occur. We have to be more precise in our language, meanings, and dialogue. It is important to note that there is no one homosexual type anymore than there is one typical heterosexual. In both worlds, there is a spectrum of feelings and behaviors. Our sexual roles and the degree to which we experience male or female attraction vary from person to person and from time to time during our lives. In 1953, Alfred Kinsey tried to illustrate this by describing a continuum on a scale of 0 to 6, with 0 indicating exclusively heterosexual orientation, and 6 referring to exclusively homosexual attraction.

Few people are exclusively heterosexual in terms of having no affectionate feelings for persons of their own sex. Most of us would find ourselves between the scale of 1 and 5, and the majority of us 1 or 2. There is a midpoint category called *bisexual*. Bisexual persons experience erotic attraction toward persons of both sexes. Considering this scale, it becomes even clearer that when we speak about homosexuality, we must be aware of the range of feelings. We need to specify whether we are referring to an orientation (that most medical scientists believe we do not choose) or a behavior (over which we do have choice).

We also need to keep the issue of homosexuality in perspective. Homosexuality is only a small part of the sexuality issues that should concern us. It is not, nor should it be, *the big issue* or even *the* sexuality issue for Christians. So often, after I speak to groups on sexuality, the first question raised in the discussion period is about homosexuality. That issue then takes up the remainder of the period. Perhaps we do that because it is safer to talk about other persons "out there." On other sexuality issues, the discussion gets too close to home, too close to our inner sexual selves, where we may feel insecure.

Actually, we who are heterosexuals have a tremendous agenda of sexuality issues of our own with which we should and must be working. Even in the church, we observe a steady decline in the level of commitment required for marriage. In the church we have sexual abuse, incest, marital rape, pregnancy outside of marriage, and a steadily increasing rate of casual sexual intercourse outside of marriage.

Some church members purchase or view pornographic materials. Television and much of the rock music industry are damaging our witness. We observe the "scoring" mentality in the dating practices of some Christian young people. We have adultery, sexism, and the chronic problem of men and women viewing each other primarily as potential sex mates and as bodies, rather than as persons, as friends, or as brothers and sisters in the church.

Yet we focus so much of our attention and wrath on homosexuality. Why are we more offended by "unnatural sex" (homosexual activity) than we are about aggressive, uncaring, exploitative "natural sex"? Many Christians whose own heterosexual behavior is crude and exploitative, who are unable to talk about their own attitudes with even a spouse, get hostile and emotional when the subject of homosexuality arises. Even though this kind of emotional reaction is a reality, most people can agree on many aspects of the homosexuality issue.

Areas of General Consensus

The following are points on which we generally do agree, or at least should be able to agree:

1. There is much diversity among homosexuals. There is no stereotype that fits all. There is no typical homosexual anymore than there is a typical heterosexual.

2. We usually cannot identify by dress, mannerisms, or speech who is same-sex oriented. Even psychological testing may fail to identify that individual. Homosexual persons do have in common their experience of discrimination; for that reason, most are closeted and invisible (not recognized as such). Gay persons are truck drivers, football players, farmers, policemen, clerks, and homemakers. They are in the professions and many other areas of endeavor. They are our relatives, friends, co-workers, and people with whom we worship in many of our congregations. If we say we do not know any gay persons, it is almost certain that we are just unaware that we do know gay persons.

3. We can agree that we should not define gay persons by their sexual orientation. Joe is a pastor, Jane is a teacher, and Pete is a farmer; but Henry is a homosexual, or Sally is a lesbian! Although our sexuality is a pervasive dimension of who we are, it is not the sole or defining dimension of our lives, whatever our orientation. I am known as a physician; let us define Henry and Sally according to their character and their roles in society as well, rather than as homosexuals.

4. It is difficult to be accurate regarding the incidence of homosexuality. It had been estimated from the Kinsey studies that from 2 to 4 percent of women and 5 to 10 percent of men are same-sex oriented, depending on how one defines homosexuality along the Kinsey scale. These percentages are being questioned today and are probably greatly inflated. In fact, many parts of the Kinsey research methods are being challenged today. It is unlikely that we can acquire accurate data because so many gay persons are closeted and have not come out publicly, justifiably fearing discrimination and even violence.

5. Homosexuals are not the "scum of the earth." Famous persons who reputedly have been gay include Erasmus, Leonardo da Vinci, Michelangelo, T. E. Lawrence, Willa Cather, William James, Queen Mary II, Walt Whitman, Tchaikovsky, Frederick the Great, Sir Francis Bacon, and Christopher Marlowe. In modern times as well, we are learning of well-known, contributing persons who are of same-sex orientation. The world has been enriched in the past and is being enriched today by the contributions of homosexual persons.

6. Homosexual orientation is not contagious. We do not "catch" it by associating with homosexual persons. It is important for people to understand that neither adults nor children are at risk of acquiring a same-sex affinity in school, church, or elsewhere from colleagues, teachers, or others.

7. Homosexual persons are not per se molesters of children, nor are they predominantly violent. In fact, most are quite the opposite—very gentle persons.

8. One same-sex erotic experience does not define one as homosexual. There is that broad spectrum of sexual preference; during our lifetimes, we move back and forth along this continuum. There is much needless anguish among persons who at some time (often in adolescence or while in an all-male or all-female environment such as single-sex colleges, the military, or prison) had an erotic homosexual experience and fear that it defines them for life. It is not helpful for the sexually obsessed media culture of our day to prey as it does on the sexual identities and sexual attitudes of insecure adolescents and to imply that people thereby "discover" who they are.

9. Not all homosexual persons want to change their core sexual attraction. Some try to change; many do not. Some consult psychiatrists or other therapists; some never do and do not want to.

10. We should be aware that many homosexuals are married to persons of the other sex and are often parents. Frequently they have married in an attempt to prove to themselves that they are not gay. They probably tried to avoid societal discrimination or to live up to family expectations. Many of these marriages eventually dissolve.

11. There are many homosexual people in our churches—often hidden, hurting, and afraid.

12. Although we do not know the cause of same-sex orientation (see next section), most people agree, based on research and the life stories of homosexual persons, that it is usually not a consciously chosen condition anymore than heterosexuality is consciously chosen. Although many in the religious community dispute this, much evidence is otherwise. Again, we do make choices on what behavior we follow.

In spite of these many points about homosexuality on which most people can agree, there are also some where people strongly disagree.

Points of Continuing Disagreement

The following three major points of disagreement are present in the church and in general society:

1. As noted above, the *causes of same-sex orientation* are not known. There are various theories. Some believe it represents a developmental arrest around the age of puberty. Others believe it is caused by some hormonal abnormality yet unidentified. Some say it is genetically caused and that someday we will discover the gene for homosexuality. Some believe it is environmentally caused, arising out of disorder in family dynamics.

There is no agreement in the medical-scientific community as to the cause of homosexuality, but there seems to be increasing evidence that there is at least a genetic link of varying degree. Studies on twins and other research suggest that homosexuality is inborn in some way, but nothing conclusive has been determined.

If there is a majority opinion, it would be that the causes of same-sex orientation are multiple and complex, and that a combination of factors along with a genetic predisposition is responsible. Dr. Verle Headings, a geneticist at Howard University, has given much study to this issue. He describes the cause of homosexuality as involving many factors and possibly various genetic origins (1024).

If this is true, it is reasonable to deduce that there is such a complex set of causative factors that the cause may differ from person to person. Perhaps that is why we hear such varying reports from both the religious and the psychiatric community as to its changeability. Possibly, because of its varying causation, some gay persons can change and others cannot, but the depth of change again would vary. Instead of saying homosexuality, perhaps we should say homosexualities.

2. Closely related to causation is the second point of disagreement: *Is same-sex orientation changeable?* Most psychiatrists say that they have seen "not one case" of permanent change of core sexual attraction of a person who is a 4, 5, or

6 on the Kinsey scale, mostly same-sex oriented. There are other psychiatrists who claim a 30 percent or more success rate in assisting persons who consult them for help in changing their sexual attraction.

Part of this discord may come from using the same word to mean different things. Are both groups of psychiatrists defining the word *change* in the same way? With many factors of causation, we can anticipate various claims of success in helping persons to change. Some define change as the ability to function sexually in a heterosexual marriage or to refrain from genital activity altogether even though the person's fantasies remain with same-sex partners. Others insist that change means a shift in one's core attraction and sexual fantasies toward persons of the other sex. Just as with causation, the changeability of sexual orientation remains unsettled and is a source of contention.

3. The third area of disagreement is over *the meaning of biblical materials* often cited as referring to homosexuality (see chapter 2, above). Sharply contrasting views persist among Bible scholars; some on both sides even demonize those who hold a different interpretation.

Jesus did not mention homosexuality, and the New Testament has only a few passages that relate to it. Scholars disagree as to whether these passages speak to the issue of gay "marriage" (between two committed, monogamous persons of the same sex in a lifelong covenant relationship). The Old Testament passages denouncing homosexual relations as an abomination also denounce other practices that we moderns routinely ignore. The Bible speaks more clearly and at much greater length on the issues of divorce, the prayer veiling, and the accumulation and use of wealth.

No language from biblical times had a word corresponding to what we term *homosexuality*. The first usage of the word *homosexuality* in an English translation was in the Revised Standard Version in 1946. In any case, any reference to same-sev eroticism is to sexual activity, not attraction. The understanding of homosexuality as a psychosexual orientation emerged late in the nineteenth century.

Those who believe the Bible speaks so clearly on this issue must remember that the texts we read have come down to us through centuries of translation and interpretation, filtered through various languages, and translated through the best efforts of biblical scholars. As Daniel Taylor says in his article, "Confessions of a Bible Translator,"

> All translation is interpretation. At every point the translator is required to interpret, evaluate, judge, and choose. Every text is thickly layered with unique and sometimes incommensurable features of form, not to mention the very sound of words. . . . This does not mean that translation is merely subjective, but we should guard against the illusion that there is a single right way of treating translation in general or any one passage in particular. (76)

In a workshop I attended, one lay church leader said, "What in the Bible seems to be plain English is often muddy Greek." Philip Yancey writes,

> Those who take up the daunting task of Bible translation step into a force field of tension. On the one hand, we must keep on arguing about proper meaning because we so highly value that meaning. On the other hand, we must recognize that all translation, indeed all language, contains an element of uncertainty. We dare not lessen the tension on either end. (88)

So what does the Bible say about homosexuality? Surely we must use a degree of humility in our pronouncements. Equally learned and sincere scholars disagree. We all have our biases and should admit them. Myron Augsburger writes,

It has been said that what any people of faith believe is not what the Bible says but what they understand the Bible to say! This is why we need to admit our perspectives. We test our perspectives by openness before the Spirit and the Word in the community of faith. (2)

It is my prayer that God will give us the spirit to grow as hearers of the Word *and* to increase our understanding of the truth through interaction and discernment with each other.

Personal Response

In view of all of the above, including the disagreements and uncertainties, what are the implications for our personal attitudes on this issue? The uncertainties and the complex dimensions surrounding the issue of homosexuality call me to sensitivity, to humility, and to compassion.

First, *sensitivity* is born out of the awareness that the person of homosexual orientation is potentially my brother or sister in Christ and, like me, is one for whom Christ died and one whom I must treat with love and respect.

Second, since there is so much about homosexuality that we do not know, I am called to *humility*. What might we learn in the next ten to twenty-five or fifty years from the Human Genome Project (mapping human genes and analyzing human DNA), from biblical scholarship, or from other research? Church people should be wary of making dogmatic pronouncements about the causation or changeability of same-sex attraction, bringing discredit on themselves if later valid research proves them wrong.

For example, if the genetic component of causation is greater than now known, how would that alter our attitudes toward gay marriage? In addition, a broader grasp of the whole of biblical teachings and of God's intention in the original creation and in the new creation may bring us more insight as we listen to each other (Hays; Grenz). Thus, our understanding of the causation, changeability, and the biblical materials is incomplete; this should lead us into an attitude of humility.

Humility is also needed because we who are heterosexual people cannot imagine what it is like to walk in the shoes of our homosexual brother or sister. Lewis Smedes put it this way: "Let it just be said, then, that no matter how sure some heterosexual people are in their moral judgments, they make them in a fog of ignorance about the deeper goings on in a homosexual's life" (64).

Third, I am called to *compassion*. I know of few other issues that have caused such suffering. I must have compassion—

1. For youngsters who grow up feeling different and do not know why.

2. For the adolescent who has almost accidentally experienced a same-sex orgasm and is tormented by the fear that he or she might be homosexual.

3. For gays who are afraid their parents will not accept them if they know of their same-sex attraction.

4. For parents who are in torment when they discover the same-sex attraction of their son or daughter and are plagued by the question, "Where did we go wrong?"

5. For parents who do not accept their gay child and rupture a parent-child relationship that should be one of unconditional love.

6. For gay persons who married in an attempt to change their sexual interest, an attempt that failed.

7. For the spouse of the gay person who does not *know* the orientation of that person in bed beside him or her and cannot understand the lack of sexual interest and the rejection being experienced in the relationship.

8. For the spouse who is locked into a marriage with a homosexual mate and worries about the effect of it on their children.

9. For the husband or wife of the gay spouse who has decided to no longer deny his or her sexual attraction and wants

out of the marriage.

10. For the children and the spouse in a family that has broken up because of the departure of a gay parent and spouse.

11. For all those in closets, unable to reveal and share who they really are.

12. For the closeted gay person who has experienced rejection, but for obvious reasons cannot seek understanding or care from pastor, parents, or anyone in their usual support system.

13. For all those who fear their sexuality, are insecure about their own sexual attractions and fantasies, and therefore indirectly influence others to remain in closets.

14. For single people who are assumed by others to be gay just because they never married.

15. For same-sex friends who cannot be carefree in their normal nonsexual friendship for fear of what people will imagine or infer. Close friends of the same sex find it difficult to form deeply bonded, nonerotic relationships; this is one of the saddest casualties of today's politicized and angrily divided society. Such relationships should be encouraged and affirmed.

16. For gays who are trying to "change" and cannot.

17. For gays who have "changed" and are called liars by their gay peers.

18. For the homosexual in the pew beside us who listens year after year to harsh utterances from TV preachers and even our own pastors, as well as to the snide remarks and cruel jokes we tell while never suspecting the sexual affinity of the person beside us.

19. For pastors who are hurting because they do not understand why a certain member does not confide in him or her, not suspecting it is because that person is gay and cannot forget the sermon condemning homosexuality two months ago.

20. For pastors who are perplexed and frustrated in dealing with gays in their congregations.

21. For church leaders who are trying to bring understanding and healing to the homosexuality discussion but who ex-

perience angry criticism for their efforts.

22. For all who are so insecure in their sexuality, in their sexual bodies, in their sexual identities, that this becomes such an explosive issue.

Need we go on? When I consider the issue of homosexuality, I am called to *sensitivity, humility,* and *compassion*.

There is an even more personal task for each of us. We need to know some homosexual persons and relate to them. We need to seek out some gay persons and become their friends. Father Richard Rohr in an audiotaped presentation, "Sexuality: The Search for Wholeness," refers to a statue of Christ at a cathedral in Chicago on which appears the inscription, "I know you and I love you." If we know someone well enough, we can love them. If we really learn to know them and visit their inner thoughts and feelings, we find that we will love them.

Observations and Future Tasks for Christians

As a starting point in resolving the tensions surrounding the issue, it is essential to *examine our attitudes* regarding homosexuality. When our attitudes reflect intolerance, hatred, or fear, we must realize how destructive and disabling they are to the one who exhibits them, as well as to the ones who are the object of them. Our gay brothers and sisters are worthwhile persons, and we owe them Christian love. A people committed to love and justice must be against discrimination and oppression of gay persons.

We can have no part in anti-gay demonstrations. We must protest and reject the attitudes of so-called Christians who display bumper stickers such as "Kill a Queer for Christ," or who carry signs that say, "God Hates Fags." We cannot join so-called Christians who oppose gay civil rights, which they call "damnable laws sure to hasten America's doom." Christ had much to say about oppression, and a people of justice can have no part in the oppression of gay people.

Second, we will have to learn to *live with some uncertainty and ambiguity.* The causes of same-sex attraction are unlikely to be known next week or next year. It is hard to live with ambiguity—we want to know everything "for sure." Uncertainty makes us uneasy and tends to give us a feeling that everything is coming unglued. We think that if we accept any new understandings, then everything is up for grabs and anything goes. I disagree. Throughout our lives, we have to deal with life on a moral slippery slope where not everything is clearly right or wrong.

On this slippery slope, we must make moral decisions from the best information and counsel available to us in discernment with fellow believers and in communion with God and the Holy Spirit. Uncertainty should lead us, in humility, into prayer and Bible study and into dialogue with those with whom we may disagree, discerning God's will *in community* under the guidance of God's Spirit. We must examine more than facts and doctrine; we must also examine our attitudes.

Third, when it comes to sexuality issues, we should always *remember that we are all vulnerable.* Who of us has a perfectly clean conscience when it comes to our sexuality? We must be careful about judging others. When we read the New Testament, we note that Jesus certainly condemned unrighteousness, but his harshest words were for the self-righteous and their arrogance (Matt. 7:1-5). We tend to single out sexual transgressions as somehow being uniquely sinful. God's grace and forgiveness encompass sexual transgressions.

In an address at Goshen College some years ago, Dr. Lewis Penhall Bird said,

> Many Christians seem to assume that the seven deadly sins were fornication, adultery, homosexuality, masturbation, venereal disease, oral-genital stimulation, and abortion. In reality, of course, they were pride, envy, anger, sloth, avarice, gluttony, and lust. All of us must seek the grace of God.

Fourth, we need to *work for church unity and fellowship.* When it comes to homosexual genital relationships, most Christian groups count this as sin. The major issue being debated has to do with the few persons who want to be a part of the church, who are eligible on all other grounds, but who are involved in a loving, committed, covenantal, and permanent relationship (like marriage) with someone of the same sex. Congregations have differed in their response. I think it is sad when that diversity in response is the cause of breaking Christian fellowship.

We have not broken fellowship with those with whom we disagree on business practices and ethics, on the payment of war taxes, on registration for the draft, on lavish versus simple lifestyles, on the use of alcohol, and on many other issues. Instead, on these issues we keep talking, searching, praying, and striving for the will of God.

Although the issue of homosexuality tends to be divisive, must it be a matter over which we divide our communions? Personally, I hope not. I believe that, mindful of the inexhaustible grace of God, we need to work responsibly on divisive issues and seek God's will in both our lifestyles and our discernment processes. This will enable us to maintain fellowship with our fellow believers.

Fifth, we also must *call the homosexual community to Christian attitudes and expression.* The homosexual community, as well as the heterosexual community, must face the task of understanding the foundations of heterosexuals' fear and behavior. Closed minds and bigoted attitudes are not helpful whether displayed by homosexuals or by heterosexuals. If we have attitudes of openness and of seeking truth instead of militant attitudes, we are more likely to understand both sides.

In addition, homosexuals should not expect the church to accept a lesser moral standard from them than it does from its heterosexual members. The church can and should have the same attitude toward sexual promiscuity, for example, whether this involves homosexual or heterosexual persons. It is expected that homosexual people monitor and discipline their thoughts and their behavior. They must hold themselves to the same moral standard that is expected of heterosexual people.

Sixth, honestly *searching for guidance* regarding the issue of homosexuality *may not bring total agreement*. However, we should be able to come together in a resolve to find new ways to live out Micah 6:8. We need a renewed commitment to "act justly and to love mercy and to walk humbly with [our] God."

This chapter encourages us to—

- view homosexuality in the context of our overall sexuality.
- narrow the areas of disagreement.
- avoid becoming emotionally bogged down with rhetoric in areas where there is no real disagreement.
- use precise language.
- emphasize the importance of our attitudes.
- affirm those who have the integrity to deal with this tough question and hear all sides.
- not break fellowship with those with whom we disagree.

If we withdraw from the struggle of wrestling and discernment, we close the door for possible transformation on either side. This transformation may come through the interaction and openness to which we say we are committed. It is clear that Christian people of goodwill have strong differences on this issue. Our task is to continue to work through it together in loving dialogue.

Discussion Questions

1. If your son or daughter would announce to you that he or she is a homosexual or a lesbian, how would you respond?
2. Why is the homosexuality issue so emotionally explosive in society? In Christian congregations and denominations?

3. We often hear that we should "hate the sin but love the sinner." How have you befriended both homosexuals and heterosexuals in your congregation?

4. Do you feel called to sensitivity, humility, and compassion with regard to same-sex orientation and toward gay persons who claim salvation through Christ? At what points do you agree or disagree with the author?

5. If you are homosexual, are you able to forgive and love those who oppress you by attitude and words?

6. When sincere Christians disagree on interpretation of Scripture, what principles can help us to stay in loving dialogue with each other?

8

The Gift and Cross-Gender Friendships

Willard S. Krabill

IN HER EXCELLENT book *How Can a Man and a Woman Be Friends?* Mary Rosera Joyce asks, "Is it *possible* for a boy and a girl [or] a man and a woman to be friends?" The question implies correctly that sexual difference in our society can be an obstacle to friendship. Friendship involves a bond between equals; throughout most of history, this kind of bond between a man and a woman was considered unlikely.

Surveys show that most people see same-sex friendship as different from other-sex friendships. Friendships between women and men are viewed as more complicated because of potential sexual tensions, for one thing. We tend to turn to our same gender for friendship and turn to the other gender for validation of our worth or desirability; for union, gratification, and possession; or even for conquest. However, men and women still strive to find friendship in their relationships with each other as well.

Qualities of True Friendship

In her book, Joyce lists four qualities of true friendship, especially "other sex" friendship: *equality, esteem, affection,* and *shared values*. Think about those four terms. It becomes evident that some male-female relationships, even marriages, are not based on friendship.

Although sexual difference affects friendship, it need not and must not be an obstacle in forming friendships if we are to

achieve healthy sexuality, experience vital female-male companionship, and understand each other's feelings and needs.

We need to understand our sexuality and our common need for intimacy and learn how to be friends. These accomplishments will help us form a society where it is usual and normal to have as many friends of the other sex as it is to have friends of our own sex. Such a society would be a place where one can feel safe to risk vulnerability or risk falling in love.

We would not need to fear dating a friend. In a climate of male-female friendship (with equality, esteem, affection, and shared values), sexual oppression and exploitation would surely diminish. One would not try to discover how far one could go in making out with a friend, or hang nude pictures of a real friend, or join in joking about the body of a friend.

Myths About Friendship

One of the myths about friendship is that friends always agree with one another. In his book, *On Being a Friend,* Eugene Kennedy says learning how to disagree with a friend begins when one realizes it is not a matter of winning or losing. By recognizing and respecting a friend's point of view, one can learn how to handle differences. Winning and losing are not applicable in friendship.

We need not always agree, but we do need always to listen—as equals who are respected and held in esteem, with affection and sharing of values. Without becoming defensive, men must listen to women's pain from living as part of an oppressive system. Women must listen to men's pain from also living as part of an oppressive system, without blaming or accusing them.

Although complete and constant agreement is not a requirement for female-male friendship, listening and equality are. We have to approach a friendship from equal power bases, fully respecting the worth and the personhood of the other. Clinging or grasping, manipulating, using, dominating or submitting, going along with love to get sex (as men tend to do), and going along with sex to get love (as women tend to do)—these do not characterize the relationship of friends.

Instead, we need to be together in a relationship of trust and respect, with equality, esteem, affection, and shared values. These qualities describe true friendship, healthy sexual friendship, and the kind of relationship out of which romance may or may not grow. In this instance, when I say romance, I am talking about a serious relationship whose foreseeable objective is permanent union.

In any case, however, a romantic relationship that over time evolves out of a friendship with this kind of integrity, is a relationship that need not be feared as a threat to friendship. It can be a romantic relationship with a far-better chance of survival than a dating relationship that short-circuits true friendship and intimacy, prematurely moves to the physical and the genital, overloads the circuits, and blows the fuse. After experiencing a few such negative episodes, one naturally becomes afraid: afraid to risk, afraid to trust, and even afraid to date.

A healthy sexuality is one that is emotional, mental, relational, and spiritual as well as physical. The physical does not necessarily include the genital relationship; that, I believe, can fulfill its potential for ecstasy only after all other dimensions of friendship, intimacy, and commitment have been achieved. A well-developed sexuality is centered in the head and soul, not in the groin. Even genital sex is not truly human without the elements of love, freedom, responsibility, decision, imagination, sensitivity, and feeling. These all are qualities of the brain, not the gonads.

Some of us have learned about sexuality and other-sex relationships from exemplary models of devoted, loving parents and extended families, and thereby we are blessed. But too many people have learned about sex and sexuality in homes where parents were not friends, were absent, had multiple partners, or modeled infidelity in various ways. Parents may have been abusive, uncles guilty of incest, and on and on. Not all have had the privilege of discovering sex in beautiful and nonexploitive ways.

Surely most of us have learned much about distorted exploitive sex as purely physical passion from the popular culture—visual and written media, music, and various examples. True male-female friendships should enable us to hear the pain of those whose learning about sex was not ideal. Such friendships should enable the already wounded among us to learn that there are women who are not out to exploit us, and men who are not out to abuse us.

Given the popular culture, it is a tremendously difficult task to grow into friendships with the other sex, relationships that enable us to fulfill our real intimacy needs. Immature and underdeveloped sexual beings seem to believe that the center of our sexuality is not in our heads but in our groins. This mentality perpetuates the false notion that a healthy female and male who are attracted to each other must either head for bed or frustrate their sexuality. Whatever happened to friendship? A genital-centered view of sexuality binds us in our erotic desires and feelings. But a person-centered view of sexuality frees us for equality and friendship.

We live in an age of compulsive sex. If we are to be freed from the enslavement of compulsive sex, we need to experience true sexual freedom. Men are not really just hungering for women's bodies. Women are not really just hungering for men's bodies. Not really! This can become a dimension of intimate relating, but the real need is for the broader fulfillment of intimacy, closeness, and friendship. True sexual friends are able to touch and hold each other in affirmation without becoming erotically aroused. To be able to do that is sexual freedom.

Friendship as Prelude to Marriage

In the context of our many friendships with persons of the

other sex, it may be that after developing a friendship, a couple will choose to marry. That chosen marriage is made secure and great by the quality of the couple's friendship. Their commitment growing out of such a friendship gives their genital union an intensity and a joy not otherwise possible.

A new sense of self and of female-male relationships can be discovered and developed. It is part of our human and God-given potential, and the rewards are astounding. In Matthew 5:27-29 and 6:22-23, Jesus emphasizes the importance of the eye, of seeing rightly, and of the relation between seeing and lust. These verses confirm that it is important how we view each other—as objects or as persons, as friends or as sex mates.

Jesus models for us what it means to be a friend. He infuses friendships with the meaning that makes them true, intimate, and worthwhile. The New Testament presents a model of head-centered, soul-centered sexuality. The greatest value two friends can share is their mutual friendship with God. Love for God intensifies human intimacy and all other qualities of friendship.

Freedom to Be Cross-Gender Friends

Why should we allow a sexually distorted society to define our sexuality and our ways of relating? Martin Luther King Jr. inspired us with his dream of equality and freedom in his famous "I Have a Dream" speech to massed thousands in Washington, D.C., August 28, 1963. I too have a dream of a society where men and women feel free to be friends, intimate friends, able to relate in equality, esteem, affection, and sharing of values without feeling any necessity or compulsion to become genital sex partners. I have a dream of a society where men and women would have as many close friends of the other sex as they do of their own sex.

I have a dream of a society where men would not tolerate for a minute the violence done to their women friends by those who rate the bodies of the women walking by. So many gutless, silent men allow such verbal garbage to go unchallenged. I dream of a society whose women are truly liberated and assertive enough to insist they are ready and available for friendship, but not for conquest by the friend. I dream of a society whose men are truly liberated and assertive enough to insist that they are ready and available for friendship, but not for possession or seduction by the friend.

I have a dream of a society where women will not feel driven to find their identity in a man; where both men and women have their relationships centered in meaning and values, in friendship and not in ownership; where women and men share friendships that promote personal growth and transcend rigidly defined roles; where men and women find joy, fun, laughter, and celebration in the company of their friends—friends who do not have to be their party mates or their sex mates.

I have a dream of a society of persons freed from genital preoccupation, who have grown enough in their sexuality to discover that the center of their sexuality is in their heads, not below their belts. I dream of a society where administrative authority is shared, in friendship, between women and men. I have a dream of a society of sexually free persons, free to enjoy their mutual attraction for each other without having to express it in an erotic or genital way. That is real sexual friendship, real sexual freedom, appropriate male-female relating.

What would fulfillment of this dream mean? It would mean the same thing it meant to Martin Luther King Jr. decades ago in Washington, D.C.: "Free at last! Free at last! Thank God Almighty, we are free at last!"

Guidelines for Developing Friendships with Other-Sex Persons Who Are Not One's Spouse

I base these guidelines on an assumption that if one is married, the relationship is solid; an atmosphere of trust and confidence exists, based on conviction and on our past performance earning that trust. The guidelines, developed from various sources, are presented as questions to ask oneself in evaluating other-sex friendships with anyone not one's spouse.

1. Is the friendship about something outside ourselves? That is, is it a shared interest about art, music, business, sports, church life, theology, or something else? If the friendship is not around some *thing*, but rather about *us*, then we are getting into a dangerous area where red flags should be raised.

2. Is it an exclusive friendship, or could it be shared with a third or even a fourth party who also is interested in the *thing* that brought us together as friends? If it is exclusive and could not be opened to a third party, we are clearly dealing with a high-risk situation.

3. Is it an equal friendship? In this relationship, is either person in an advantageous position over the other? Is either trying to impress the other or manipulate the other for any purpose? If one party to the friendship has an advantage or is trying to impress or manipulate the other, there is danger.

4. Can we talk openly with others about our relationship, or is it secret? Do we have to hide the fact that we are friends with the other person and are meeting with the other person to share a relationship? Secretive friendships are risky.

5. Is the activity we share and our behavior within the relationship appropriate to friendship rather than courtship? Is it clear and assumed (discussed if need be) that sexual attraction is not acted upon? The friendship must be considered too important to let a sexual undertow drown it.

6. If we are married, does the relationship add to or take away from our respective marriages? Could our spouses be invited along or invited to look on at any time? Would our behavior be the same if our spouses were present? If not, there is danger.

7. Am I jealous of this friend? If so, the relationship is suspect.

8. Do I *need* the relationship, or do I *want* the relationship?

Is the friendship something I enjoy and desire, or is it *necessary* for my emotional needs to be met? If I *need* the other person, again we are dealing with a risky situation; the friendship needs to be reevaluated and reconstituted on a different basis. We should be able to say, "I appreciate you, but I do not *need* you."

Discussion Questions

1. What might contribute to forming a person-centered view of sexuality that frees us for equality and friendship, rather than a genital-centered view that binds us in our erotic desires and feelings?
2. Some people relate more easily with people of the other gender than with those of their own gender. What factors contribute to this? What factors make this difficult for others?
3. How can fulfillment of the dream to have intimate friends in both genders be facilitated and promoted?
4. What steps should one take when the answers to questions asked in the guidelines raise dangerous warnings?

9

The Gift and the Sensuous

Anne Krabill Hershberger

CAN WE SERIOUSLY consider sensuousness to be a divinely approved aspect of God's gift of sexuality? Augustine of Hippo and other church leaders, drawing on the dualisms of their cultures, effectively convinced Christians that body and soul were distinctly separate entities in the human being, and that the soul was good and the body was bad. Ever since, we have had a hard time accepting what we experience through our bodily senses as positive contributors to human well-being.

This tragic error has been countered in recent decades with new insights about the wholeness of human beings—an integration of body, mind, and spirit. However, we still do not give much public credence to the positive role sensuous experiences can have in our relationships with each other.

We know the biblical story of the woman whose tears fell on Jesus' feet. She then wiped his feet with her hair before pouring expensive perfume on him (Luke 7:36-39, 44-50). As we ponder this drama, we have often been led to think about the economic issues related to her act. She used this extravagantly expensive way of doing what was otherwise culturally common in that day, washing the feet of guests as an expression of hospitality.

Simon, the host of the occasion, had failed to offer this common act of hospitality when Jesus arrived. But he was quick to suggest that the perfume the woman used should have been sold and the money given to the poor. He saw excess and waste in the woman's expression of her love for Jesus.

Less often have we given thought to the meaningful, sensuous impact this act likely had on Jesus. Here is the *visual* image of a caring woman whose love for Jesus moved her to tears, whose long hair was used to express her love through *touch*, and whose perfume filled the room with pleasant *fragrance*. In Matthew's account of this story, Jesus said, "She has done a beautiful thing to me." He promised that wherever the gospel is preached throughout the world, this story would be told and her memory would be perpetuated (Matt. 26:6-13).

Our culture has given *the sensuous,* qualities that appeal to the senses, a bad name among Christians because of the way the culture exploits what should be beautiful and reduces it largely to *the sensual,* gratification of physical appetites. People are often presented in a sensual way, as ends in themselves, or to sell products or distorted values.

Instead of portraying males and females with all their diverse and interesting characteristics, our society promotes a stereotypical image that few can realistically emulate. Society's message is that we, especially women, are not acceptable unless we "fix" ourselves—skin, size, hair, lips, eyes, nails, breasts, clothes. . . .

In various media, scantily clad women with pouting expressions and well-toned, weight-lifting men perpetuate stereotypical sensual images. Much as we may resist this kind of presentation of the human, we cannot deny that sensory experiences are meaningful to us in many ways; they can be particularly significant in our relationships with each other.

Most people find spiritual uplift in the *sensuous* experience of being in a natural setting and viewing the beauty of flowers, trees, streams, animals, mountains, rocks, and the rest of God's creation. As we feel the wind against our skin while running, biking, or sailing, we sense goodness in our lives.

We also recognize the spiritually enriching experience of seeing, hearing, and/or participating in thoughtfully conceived, effectively communicated, and well-crafted artistic expressions in the areas of fine art, music, theatre, and dance. But all these examples do not reflect how our senses can serve us well in our relationships with others.

As affirmed above, we are all sexual beings all of the time, and we relate to each other sexually in all our interactions—some of us as females and some as males. Again, we are referring to sexual relating much more broadly than the act of sexual intercourse. What role does sensuousness play in these nonspecific sexual relationships?

What different people consider pleasing to their senses will vary significantly. Yet in general, most people will respond well to others who take the time and trouble to be clean and well-groomed and who wear attractive, well-fitted clothing. The narrator in the film *The Sexiest Animal* says that human beings are the only animals able to choose their own plumage—and do we ever choose plumage (clothes)! Fine weaves, coarse weaves, bright colors, dark colors, soft and silky, hard surface and bulky, formal design and casual style, clothes made for action, and clothes made for ceremonies of dignity.

What can be sensuous about all this is the appropriateness and attractiveness of how we present ourselves. We are drawn to people who care enough about themselves and others to enhance the human landscape by presenting themselves in the most-attractive way they know and can muster.

It is important to take seriously the biblical admonition in Matthew 6:31 not to worry about what we shall eat, drink, and wear. The body is more important than clothing. However, carefully selected clothing fabric, design, and fit can accentuate our positive features and be an aesthetically pleasing "gift" to the people with whom we relate. This gift can express Christian principles. Well-fitting and well-chosen clothing sends a more important message than expensive, high-fashion clothing. Clothes need not be the latest style to please the senses, but neither do they need to defy contemporary design.

More potentially pleasing to the senses than our clothing is the body language and social graces we use in each interpersonal encounter. There can be something quite sensuous about a friendly smile, handshake, hug, and direct eye contact while maintaining respect for one's personal space.

Positive sensations come to us when persons with whom we are in conversation are not easily diverted by the presence or activities of other people in the area. We show respect for a dialogue partner if we refuse to put aside the current focus when "more-important" people come into view. Introducing each person in the immediate environment and kindly excusing oneself when needing to leave a conversation—such things all have something to do with sensuousness. They *feel* good.

Not everything that *feels* good is appropriate, however. Caring about one's personal appearance and developing social skills require discipline to avoid two extreme attitudes. Some people tend to criticize the efforts of others who try to present themselves in positive ways, almost priding themselves in appearing in nonpleasing ways and behaving in a socially inept manner. At the other extreme, some people seem to flaunt their physical bodies and apparel, send inappropriately tempting and sexually seductive messages, and exude an almost smothering "friendliness" when relating to others. Neither attitude nor behavior becomes a Christian.

For a Christian whose life is focused on allowing Christ's love to flow through self to others, the senses are key in this communication. Loving touch, caring eye contact, empathetic listening, fragrant flowers, or tastefully prepared food—these all send a message: "You, my friend, matter to me. You are worthy to receive love." How beautiful! How sensuous!

Let us move from the arena of general human interactions to a specific relationship that holds romantic meaning for the individuals involved. The level of sensuous expression also is likely to become more intense. A dating relationship often is initiated by sensory stimuli: "the sound of his voice," "that wonderful smile of hers when our eyes meet." When two people enjoy each other's company and are most happy when they are together, opportunity exists for them to develop a relationship of true intimacy, with all the ingredients described in chapter 3.

Here again, the senses play an important role in the relationship. The conversation as well as the type of touching will become more personal. At this stage, before experiencing intense degrees of passion, it is so important for the dating pair to decide how far to allow physical interaction to go. It is no secret that couples often find touch communicating their deepest feelings for each other in ways that words cannot.

Consider the following levels of commitment. Make two photocopies of the form (on the next page). Ponder the degree of physical interaction with which you are comfortable and which you think is appropriate for each type of relationship.

On one form, record the letter before each of the physical expressions in the "self" column beside the level of commitment where you believe it best fits. Ask your friend to do the same in the "friend" column of another copy of the form.

Compare your responses. Do you agree in your opinions? Discuss your differences before you find yourselves in the heat of passion. This could be very important to your relationship and to your lives.

How can the gift of sensuousness bring joy and be an enhancement to the sexual relationship of a married couple, committed to each other for life? When beginning a relationship with another person, none of us know what life experiences will come to us. Some of these may bring dramatic life changes, with potential for great joy or for major distress. However, one of the greatest threats to a satisfying long-term sexual relationship may actually be a lack of drama in the relationship—a sameness or routine year in and year out. Creative sensuous experiences are important in fostering a deepening appreciation for each other.

Popular magazines present many articles and suggestions to prevent or respond to monotony in a long-term relationship.

One often sees advice like "put more sizzle or excitement into your marriage" or "surprise him/her tonight." The specific suggestions given by the popular media as to how this can be done may or may not fit with Christian values, but the basic concept is important. Creative use of the sensuous is significant.

Levels of Commitment	Self	Friend	Physical Expressions of Affection
Casual attraction			a. Holding hands, light embracing
Good friends, non-monogamous			b. Casual, closed-mouth kissing
			c. Intense, open-mouth kissing
Going steady, monogamous			d. Horizontal embrace, clothed
			e. Above the waist petting, clothed
Considering engagement			f. Above the waist petting, unclothed
			g. Below the waist petting, clothed
Announced engagement			h. Below the waist petting, unclothed
			i. Nude embrace
			j. Oral-genital sex
Marriage			k. Sexual intercourse

The sensuous experiences that mean so much in the dating relationship need to be continued in marriage, but in new and perhaps unpredictable ways. In their book *Sizzling Monogamy,*

Earl and Rose Smith use the term *comfort zone* to analyze what happens at different times in every intimate relationship. Usually, *comfort* would sound like something desirable for which to strive. In an intimate relationship, it can mean being at ease with each other. But comfort can also mean being chronically bored with each other as you settle into everyday life and slowly let the romance in the relationship die.

The Smiths say this experience is inevitable. Yet a couple can recognize when being in the comfort zone is becoming a potential threat to the relationship and then do something about it. In their marriage seminars, they counsel many people who are looking for more-fulfilling relationships. The Smiths recommend that couples indulge in "a marital affair with their mates"—not an extramarital affair with someone outside the marriage relationship. Capitalize on the features that make an "affair" appealing. These seem to be the elements of escape from everyday routines and responsibilities and secret rendezvous in romantic settings, spawning excitement and fun.

Many books, articles, and television and radio talk show hosts have discussed how to keep the romantic spark in a marriage—how not to take each other for granted. The Christian would start with love and commitment as basic to an enduring relationship. Sometimes Christians, however, think that simply having these in place insures a happy marriage. They may give limited attention to some of the very human elements that can be so enriching to the relationship.

We humans have been given a gift of the sensuous to enjoy and therefore should not neglect it. Speakers and writers regularly make the point that arousing the senses is important and then list various elements, such as the following.

Create an uncluttered atmosphere with candlelight, beautiful music, and pleasant fragrance. Present yourself to the most-important person in your world in a way that says that you care deeply about him or her. Such memory-making ingredients help to build a happy marriage. We can add caring conversation and true listening—not so much about life's struggles as about the richness of life together. Thereby we can enrich the soft caresses, kissing, and physical expression of love. We add to the excitement when we have fun creating such intimate times and building into them some mystery and anticipation and perhaps a bit of mischief.

Is there a place for the sensuous when Christians relate as sexual beings with each other? Indeed there is. Are there boundaries to respect in expressing and satisfying our sensuousness? Of course there are. Is it possible to control our human appetites for sensual stimulation? Yes, it is not only possible but also essential that we do so, with respect for God's good gift of sexuality and the quality of our relationships.

This ability to control is part of what makes us different from other animals. It is part of what makes life more abundant and enjoyable. May God give us the insight to enjoy this good gift, enrich life for others, and honor our Creator in all our attitudes and behaviors.

Discussion Questions

1. Many authorities agree that a lack of comfort with our sexuality adds to our fear of enjoying sensuous pleasures. How can we help ourselves to become more comfortable with our sexuality and with sensuous pleasures?
2. Social graces are obviously lacking among some people, even among some Christians. How can congregations and individuals, including parents and teachers, facilitate the development of social graces in themselves and others?
3. When the "sizzle" or romance is no longer experienced in a marriage relationship by one or both partners, what might be done to help restore this?
4. When some persons exude too much "sizzle" for comfort as they relate to others, how might we respond in a helpful manner?

10

The Gift Expressed in the Arts

Lauren Friesen

WORKS OF ART and the ability of an individual to find expression in the arts have become significant factors in the development of human emotions and knowing. On a routine basis, we are exposed to many art experiences and participate in those events as spectators, creators, critics, or consumers of artistic works.

Artistic expression and viewer response involve sensuous components, even though the experience of an entire work of art is more than just a series of sensations. These sensory elements may focus on the composition of units of color, composition, sound, rhythm, and line; or even on sensuous or sexual imagery. Significant art evokes emotions that form a unified and whole experience.

Similarly, sexual arousal engages the total personality in feeling and thought. Significant art evokes from a viewer a consequent degree of response (emotive and cognitive—knowing with awareness and judgment). Repeated viewing continues to sustain or even increase the high level of attention. When sexuality, sexual images, or sexual feelings are expressed in the art, we can experience these in new ways and with enhanced understanding and appreciation for our embodied selves.

The first part of this chapter will explore the nature of artistic expression and how it can communicate. This is followed by examples of the arts expressing sexuality.

Many art forms are highly complex, such as abstract painting or symbolist theater. Others give the appearance of being more simplified and therefore more accessible to the public. But whatever the level of sophistication, there are a number of central questions that apply to all works of art. These questions center on epistemological and ontological issues—on how we know something, and on how something exists: What do we learn from the experience of art? What qualifies an object to be called a work of art?

Such questions aid in providing a framework for understanding the relationship between a work of art and its sensuousness. The sensuousness of a work of art creates an aesthetic event for the creator or observer of the work. It also serves as an analogy for meaning that is beyond (transcendent to) the work itself.

Sensuousness (Feeling) in Art

The sensuous element in art is an integral dimension in the experience of the work. Music involves sound and rhythm, painting engages the eye, poetry elicits a lively interaction between the word and cadence, and theater stimulates response from nearly all five of the human senses. These sensuous elements in art engage the mind and body in a response that is an analogy to human sexual response, says the philosopher Arthur Danto. The common bond between art and sexuality is the presence of passion, which guides much of life and thought.

These passions, so common to human experience, are a major element in artistic expression and knowing. Even though artistic knowing is not limited to emotional arousal, it certainly explores the depth of human feeling. Danto separates art from "mere" human emotion in the sense that appreciation for art is learned behavior; we acquire the ability to access the feelings in a work of art. These feelings are not in conflict with intellectual knowledge; instead, they may form the basis for rational thought, as Susanne Langer asserts (74ff.).

The artistic expression of passion is accomplished in many subtle and some not-so-subtle ways. Art is the exploration into the context of feeling and form, of passion and abstract thought. Langer claims that these two dimensions form a dialectic: one cannot be achieved without the other.

In this fashion, art fills a void in human knowing that cannot be supplied by more-cognitive disciplines, no matter how much they discuss art. That void in the knowledge of human feeling is not filled if education programs only explore cognitive disciplines. Aesthetic education provides an understanding of sensuous arousal through art; by analogy, those feelings are also aroused through human sexual response.

The artist expresses human feeling in multiple ways. As the philosopher Benedetto Croce reminds us, artistic knowing differs from other forms of knowing. Art challenges us with infinite possibilities; forms of (empirical) knowledge based on observation or experience involve the learning of finite truths. These infinite possibilities are made possible through art and are associated with the wide latitude of knowing that the artwork arouses in the viewer.

According to Croce, the more complex the sensuous and intuitive responses to an art object, the more significant the work will be (85). This perspective was already suggested by Immanuel Kant in his *Critique of Judgement* (146).

The artist explores the complexity of feeling by employing material substances, such as paper, ink, wood, metal, paint, fabric, and dyes. These objects are not the work in and of themselves, and yet the artwork could not exist without them. The artist explores the limits and possibilities of expression with mundane objects. Sometimes this results in minimal use and manipulation of objects. A painting may just use the color red and the sensuous response that red evokes. A poem may use word sounds that do not make intelligible statements.

It is a surprise to many viewers of art that such minimal works, employing so few material substances, still express an infinite range of feelings. Other works employ a wide range of substances with multiple colors, shapes, and sounds to create the desired aesthetic effect. Whether the artist has elected simple elements or complex ones for expression, the effect can be similar in the sense that our feelings may be deeply engaged by either method.

When artworks engage our feelings, we turn our sole attention to them; it is not simply in looking at a work of art but in "dwelling in" it that we become engaged with the art (Polanyi: 18). *Dwelling in* a work of art implies the capacity to withhold critical judgment until the viewer has imaginatively entered into the world that the artwork creates. Entering into a work of art opens one to be emotionally and intellectually changed by a musical composition, painting, play, or dance.

The emotions of the viewer need to become fully engaged to shift from being an analytical "observer" to being altered emotionally by the sensuous experiences the artwork provides. A relationship is formed between art object, the creator of the art, and the viewer. It is a relationship that impacts the viewer's capacity to feel and to think.

Art as Transcendence

Profound experiences of art are not limited to sensuous moments. Those works that open up worlds to the viewer-listener also, by analogy, imply an existence beyond the art object. When we engage our senses in a composition, such as Brahm's *Requiem,* we experience, not just the work itself, but also the world it creates, within which we momentarily dwell and have our being. When a work stimulates our senses at our basic level of experience, it also lifts us beyond the sensuous and into the realm of the ontological, the domain of being.

A reading of the text of the *Requiem*, while essential to the entire work, is not the experience of the musical event, which is created by hearing it produced musically. The same can be said of the musical composition too; it is neither just an assemblage of notes on paper nor a sequence of measures played by an orchestra. Instead, significant music provides a unified sensuous experience that creates an aesthetic world into which the listener enters and dwells. When we dwell in an artwork, we come to recognize a state of being and existence beyond our immediate sensory world. Our reflection on these aesthetic moments, in turn, also provides us with insight into human sensuous and sexual experiences.

The transcendent dimensions of art are dependent, though, on the experience of actual objects (in aesthetic discussions, music is a created "object"). The sensuous experience works as a whole unit and is a requirement for aesthetic experience and transformation. The transcendent dimension in aesthetics emerges from response to an artwork. Without the actual object, aesthetic experiences would be impossible.

While nature may provide beauty and pleasure, it does not thereby provide aesthetic experiences, because these moments require human-made objects. As materials are shaped and transformed into objects of meaning and significance by the artist, they become instruments for aesthetic experiences to transform human perception.

Emotional Dimension in Art

The aesthetic world is also an emotional dimension. The arts not only "cause" an emotional response in the listener, but also deal with greater complexities. Susanne Langer has outlined the possibility that artistic experiences articulate human emotions and reveal their shapes. She assumes that human feeling has been formed by cultural and artistic development, and that art reveals both the feeling and structure. Langer claims that our feelings are an "ordered" part of our beings, and that art alone gives expression to the complex connection between emotion and form (90).

According to this perspective, a work of art is a "window" to our emotions and their shapes. Works that repeatedly engage us emotionally will provide the most-profound learning experiences. We learn to recognize an emotion we may not have noticed before the artwork reveals it to us, such as the birth, growth, and death of feelings of joy, anger, or sexual response.

These feelings and their presence and power form a sensuous aspect of being human. Recognition of such feelings is the foundation for knowledge; emotion forms the basis for rational thought, Langer says. Emotions are part of human existence, an ordered dimension of our lives, and art provides a direct "window" through which we perceive and express feelings.

Art that engages the viewer will provide a significant degree of sensuous pleasure. This does not imply that it will necessarily be decorative or that all art needs to be beautiful. Art arousing sensuous pleasure provides experiences that stimulate and frequently, though not always, are pleasing to the senses. Some works of art may stimulate through unpleasant or even grotesque sensations. Even these works provide a degree of "pleasure," but not because humans enjoy the grotesque. Instead, aesthetic pleasure is derived from the depth of feeling that a work of art evokes, not in limiting the kinds of feelings.

In Victor Hugo's novel *The Hunchback of Notre Dame,* the hunchback is not a pleasant figure. Yet he envelops us with his personality, which cannot be separated from his physical deformity. The pleasure in reading this novel or seeing the movie based on it comes, not from superficial beauty, but because we emotionally dwell in the suffering of the protagonist.

In her recent play *Twilight: Los Angeles 1992*, Harvard University professor Anna Deavere Smith has portrayed key figures from the Los Angeles riot of 1992, also known as the Rodney King riot. She has created the script of the play from interviews with many participants in the riot. Smith has condensed each person's statements into a poetic form, but the language, rhythm, and tone of each character is retained.

A wide spectrum of characters inhabit this play: participants in the Reginald Denny attack, Mayor Bradley, Police Chief Gates, and many individuals from the black, Asian, Latino, and white communities. Smith performs each character and creates distinguishing features for each one: a costume piece, accent, tone of voice, rhythm, or movement.

The experience of the play is an encounter with the persons active in the riot and affected by it. This collage of personalities creates a world within which the audience can dwell and begin to feel the various emotions coming from each character. The audience is led through a landscape of emotional possibilities: anger, fear, compassion, remorse, jubilation, anger, and many more.

As the wide range of emotions and the swift alteration of personalities and impressions flow from the stage, the context and causes for the riot begin to emerge. It becomes a world unknown to many people in the audience. Yet, through the sensuous experiences of these characters and their words, the audience can enter into their experiences. The play serves as a window to the nature and depth of their feelings.

Even so, the play is more than a litany of impressions and emotions. By juxtaposing stories from various ethnic groups and organizations, Smith also provides an experience that transcends each individual story. During an evening in the theater, this play creates the context of the riot, brings it into focus, and provides foundations for new thoughts about it.

Smith does not merely vilify or excuse the rioters; this is not a lament for the victims. Instead, she presents their stories and allows us, the viewers, to dwell in their experiences so we will be able to discover new dimensions from that cataclysm. This enables the audience to make judgments about that event and avoids the simplistic tendency to moralize about the victims of urban decay.

From many different perspectives, Smith presents the feelings of pain and joy, frustration and hope, and anger and forgiveness. In doing so, she has developed a play that liberates the viewer from being ensnared by those same feelings. In this sense, art becomes transforming: it can change our feelings and thoughts about significant issues as we dwell in the artwork. Many in the audience at the Goshen College production (Mar. 1997) commented on how the play impacted their understanding of the riot and changed their feelings about it.

The poet Denise Levertov also opens up emotional worlds for the reader. She allows the experience of transformation to occur from the aesthetic experience. In this short poem, Levertov speaks of love, meaning, and loss (73):

For Steve
This morning after your midnight death,
I wake to *Lieder*—
Schumann, Schubert, the Goethe settings.
Why did I not make sure that you
(and your partner also before his death,
whose cabaret songs would perhaps
have pleased Franz Schubert) came to know this music?

This is the way
Mourning always begins to take root
And add itself to one's life. A new
Pearl-gray thread entering the weave:
This longing to show, to share,
Which runs full tilt into absence.

Here elements of love, loss, and meaning are readily identified. The deaths of Steve and his partner provide a new way of hearing Schumann and Schubert and pose a significant question: "Why did I not make sure that you came to know this music?" This regret becomes one aspect of the poet's loss that contributes to a new understanding of life as infused with a longing to share and reveal. But this longing cannot be fulfilled; it reaches a void, an absence.

When the specter of death appears, Levertov explores the complexity of loss and the accompanying regret, with a universal question about life: "Did I do all I could?" She says this not to bring physical wholeness, in this case, but to provide the pleasure of music—to open a world to them.

Her poem is also about the meaning of music in life and how art can function to establish empathy and compassion within the human community. Poetically, music becomes a cup of cold water given in time of need, the winter coat shared with a stranger on the road. The sharing of art is the act of compassion toward those who need meaning and significance in their lives.

Suddenly, as this poem moves from morning to mourning, the reader perceives the world this music has created, a realm of emotions speaking of love, loss, beauty, and regret. The words create an experience that forms a unified moment where feeling and thought intersect. They establish a series of emotions enabling the reader to take residence in the image made by the poem, even though that image shifts from line to line.

Art as Experience

The American painter Mark Rothko also wanted to make worlds in which viewers can dwell. There were times when he would sit for hours in front of an unfinished painting and become absorbed by the painted image, like a mystic contemplating the eternal. He sought for a way in which the painter could express emotions directly and evoke a similar response in the viewer.

With his large red, blue, or black canvases, he did not want to paint a "suffering figure" to illustrate the suffering of others. Neither did he paint lonely landscapes to express the feeling of isolation. Instead, he wanted an image that would lead us, the viewers, to a *feeling* of suffering or one of isolation.

By painting shapes on large canvases, he sought to have the

color itself express feeling, to stimulate a more-powerful experience than works using recognizable figures to represent a feeling. Rothko says, "People who weep before my pictures are having the same experience I had when I painted them" (Breslin: 325). He wanted the viewer to come into direct "contact" with color and thereby gain a certain feeling from the work instead of having a recognizable image as an intercessor.

This process of painting large "blocks" of color so that the viewer can dwell in them was a spiritual (transcendent) enterprise for Rothko. In my conversations with Dr. Breslin (at the University of California-Berkeley, 1994), he stated his personal belief that Rothko had intended a "spiritual" dimension for all of his work, not just his late "chapel paintings."

In the 1950s, Harvard University commissioned Rothko to paint a series of murals for the new Holyoke Center. When Nathan Pusey, Harvard president, went to New York to examine the finished works, Rothko showed him five large canvases painted in various shades of eggplant, with hints of blue, red, and pink. Rothko asked Pusey for his comments. After a long, long pause, Pusey said, "I think they are very sad."

This direct path to the emotion that Rothko wanted to portray opened the door of conversation between the artist and Pusey. After extensive dialogue, Rothko offered that the first three paintings (respectively) represented the feelings of Maundy Thursday, Good Friday, and Easter—with hints of pink for Easter expressing the glimmer of hope in resurrection. This abstract expressionist painter had grounded his work on the belief that art provides a direct experience of human emotion and, at the same time, provides the potential for a transcendent one. Art, for Rothko, was a discipline through which he explored spirituality, the shape and content of spiritual feelings.

If the arts provide meaning and value and do not exist just to decorate walls, then a pragmatic question remains: How does art accomplish this? The motif of making meaning, as Frank Kermode has so aptly stated, is the artistic act of making the invisible visible (130).

Art makes things visible by presenting objects in an altered relationship. This is the definitive element in the modern quest for meaning and value. The task for the artist and for those who view art is then an enormous one: opening windows onto life and exposing the raw emotions that reside there, as the first step in transforming what is meaningless into something meaningful.

Embracing Life Through Art

Art is unique, not only because it expresses feeling, but also because it has the capacity to explore all of life's dimensions. The ambiguities and complexities of life are recurring themes in significant art. Art has the capacity to embrace all dimensions of human experience and to provide experiences that transform the viewer and creator of the art.

The theme of sexuality, appearing early in the chapter, is a significant component in this constellation of human perception, feeling, and meaning. Whether the models in the painting or the characters on stage are nude or fully dressed, they are always rooted in their sexual identity. That fact gives significance to their words, actions, and feelings.

The sculptor who shapes the human figure with clay or bronze is exploring what many consider to be the most-daunting challenge for an artist: the rendering of the human form. Similarly, the poet who writes of a specific love or an occasion of loss, as in Levertov's poem, is opening a window and providing knowledge of love for all who elect to enter that room.

Some choose to close the portal to these direct encounters before they have an effect or even alter the viewer. The exploration into human feeling opens the possibilities that all emotions become legitimate for artistic expression, including the pleasures of the erotic.

There is a distinction, an important one, between pornography and the erotic. Pornography is an explicit act of degrading another person or that person's image. Human sexual response incorporates erotic pleasure and desires as a valid aspect of sexual expression. In comparison, as Gloria Steinem has noted, pornography is rooted in a desire to dominate or subjugate women (Francoeur: 642).

Artists have often explored various dimensions of sexual desire and expression. Plays frequently present the mutual attraction of two persons for each other and their sexual feelings. Shakespeare's *Romeo and Juliet,* where the principals do not even kiss on stage, is a love story examining the power of sexual attraction and the beauty of desire. Even the long-standing enmity between their families, the Capulets and the Montagues, is not as powerful as their desire for each other.

This power to evoke human passion has intrigued artists and audiences through the ages. As with many other artistic explorations, artists have frequently been ambivalent toward political and religious taboos on this subject or exploited those taboos. But it is not merely an intrigue with erotic passion that informs much of art focusing on sexual desire.

Significant works of art portraying the erotic dimension of sexuality are exploring the connection between the aesthetic image and the nature of human experience. This connection is a powerful one within the imagination. As Danto suggests, it combines two experiences that are highly similar: the arousal from sexual attraction with the arousal from an aesthetic experience. It is somewhat understandable that viewers who do not have an appreciation for the complexity of art will not be able to understand the connection between these similar modes of stimulation.

The playwright Ron Penhill presents erotic themes in *Love and Understanding,* viewed by this chapter writer in its premiere, at London's Shepherd's Bush Theatre, on May 27, 1997. Penhill presents the body and the erotic as metaphors for exploring the themes of love's variations and commitment.

The play contrasts two relationships: one that is kind and considerate but devoid of passion, and another that is explosive and filled with emotions.

The action of the play demonstrates how simple kindness and emotional distance eventually give way to passion and sexual desire. The characters have a moment of "understanding" when they realize that passionate attraction is at the root of commitment, and that erotic pleasures are a significant and necessary element in expressing love. The erotic themes in the play form a metaphor illuminating the search for love, conveying meaning beyond the mere appearance of the body.

The playwright might have chosen other means to express this theme, but it is significant that he chose not to do so. He presents the viewer with the challenge to dwell in the erotic and loving world of this play. As the title implies, the object is not simply to present eroticism on a stage but to provide an experience that transforms the characters and thereby also alters our understanding of human personality and love. The element of transformation through erotic awareness is at the heart of this play. The action of the play, then, is built on the risks connected with sensual love. It contrasts those feelings with the human tendency to strive toward a serene life, one lacking erotic pleasure.

In the final scene, the play does not endorse one type of love (erotic) and condemn another (serene and platonic); instead, it portrays the limitations of both. The characters come to an understanding that a committed and loving relationship is strengthened in the presence of both dimensions, passion and commitment. The characters recognize their need to be "liberated" from their previously held and limited perceptions of love and passion. They realize that healthy, passionate love requires commitment.

In the confessional conclusion, the characters acknowledge to each other their own mistakes in action and judgment. The portrayal of this disclosure enables the audience to participate in that moment of recognition. For the play, however, the confessions come too late, and the broken relationships cannot be healed. By dwelling in that disclosure, the audience is able to transform its own understanding of the connection between committed love and the presence of passion.

The play confirms Aristotle's ancient view that the depth of human feeling, when expressed in exaggerated means through art (tragedy), would lead to human wholeness (catharsis). The feelings that works of art evoke and express are closely connected with human well-being.

A contemporary writer, Martha Nussbaum, has developed this theme further. In *The Therapy of Desire* (especially the chapter "Emotions and Ethical Health"), she argues that while art does provide a sense of wholeness, it is also the foundation for ethical behavior. Humans learn to feel the distinctions between good and evil through art. An "emotional" appreciation for art serves as a form of therapy, a road to emotional health.

These examples of artistic expression are meant to illustrate the infinite and creative possibilities for gaining insight and appreciation for sexuality as a significant dimension of life. Art is also an important part of the foundation for culture and learning because it stimulates reflection (thought) and feeling (passion), while insisting that living faithfully involves the integration and expression of both. This prospect, a life centered on expressive commitment and fulfillment, is the function of art in human experience, and surely a phenomenal aspect of God's creative work in us.

Discussion Questions

1. Many thinkers have said that the arts have the capacity to communicate universally to all humans, especially across gender lines. Do you believe this? If so, why? Give examples.

2. How does art make the invisible visible? How might you

relate this to an understanding of sexuality as expressed in the arts?

3. Why does a song, painting, poem, or other art form have the capacity to move us so deeply, not only emotionally, but spiritually and physically as well? Can you recall any artwork that created such a transcendent moment for you? Why do you remember it?

4. Some works of art feature the erotic as pleasurable and constructive. How is this different from pornography and its effect in destroying human well-being?

5. Not all art that engages the viewer-participant in sensuous ways may be considered "beautiful." Do insights gained through effective and yet unattractive aesthetics allow the artwork to become "beautiful" because the insights increase your understanding? Explain your reasoning.

11

The Gift Misused

Willard S. Krabill and Anne Krabill Hershberger

IT IS CLEAR that many people are not choosing to live their lives according to God's intention. Among the greatest concerns of people in our churches and in society at large is the disturbing awareness that something has gone badly awry regarding love, sex, marriage, and commitment. All around us, we see the debris and the victims from the distortion of our sexuality.

There are many broken marriages, abortions, pregnancies of the unwed, teenage parents, and abused men and women—especially women. There is much sexual inequality and harassment, coercion, and rape. Sexually transmitted diseases abound, along with sexual ignorance and misunderstanding. Less observable but equally painful is the inner world: disillusionment experienced by teenagers and others; guilt feelings; loss of self-confidence, good reputations, and the confidence of one's mentors and friends; social discrimination; psychological damage; and lack of spiritual accountability.

We believe that our sexuality is a good gift from God. So then, why are these things happening?

In general, our society ignores or disrespects God and a Christian lifestyle. This paves the way for the development of many sexual problems. The "god" that usually claims our allegiance is a love of self and what we think will satisfy us. Then it is not a large step to disrespect other people.

Added to this is a constant bombardment of overt or covert messages to "do what feels good," "get it wherever you can," "go with the flow," "get out when the going gets rough," "show her who's boss," "score whenever and wherever you can," "be sexy or miss the good life," and on and on. We clearly have been influenced by a society obsessed with one dimension of our sexuality—the physical; people equate intimacy with sexual intercourse. That is faulty and is only the beginning of our problem with society's influence.

In Romans 12:1-2, Paul warns us,

> Don't let the world around you squeeze you into its own mold, but let God re-mold your minds from within so that you may prove in practice that the plan of God for you is good, meets all His demands, and moves toward the goal of true maturity. (Phillips)

Too often, when it comes to living our sexuality, we have not heeded this warning. We have allowed ourselves to be molded by the sexual influences of our society. When we try to identify some of the influences in our sexual understanding and mores, we rarely think first of home and church, even though these are crucially influential in many areas of our lives. When we consider current influences, we rather tend to think first of the usual culprits leading our popular culture: many stars of stage, screen, and television; parts of the music industry; and purveyors of violence, sadism, pornography, and computer sex.

We think of some advertisements with blatant and demeaning sexual innuendoes. They are culprits, to be sure, and we should keep trying to counteract their activities and messages with conviction. In their greed and selfishness, they are destroying our families, corrupting our children, objectifying women, and misusing God's gift. We could justifiably continue to indict these usual culprits, but in doing so, we would let ourselves off too easily.

Consider the societal characteristics behind these usual suspects, the factors we allow to have such influence in our lives and the lives of our children. How has the world squeezed us into its mold?

Consumerism

Consumption defines Western society. Consumer capitalism strongly influences the other values in our society. With it comes the bombardment of advertising, which coaxes us to consume more and more. Consumerism has sanctified choice—choice of new products, new brands, and new pleasures, keeping us perpetually dissatisfied. Gradually, our wants become our needs, and our needs become our demands for all kinds of temporary pleasures that we are led to believe will make us happy.

Excessive consumption of things is bad enough, but consumerism as a "character-shaping" way of life should concern us most. In *Christianity Today,* Rodney Clapp states,

> The consumer way of life fosters a number of values contrary to many Christian virtues. Can we simultaneously seek and to some degree realize both instant gratification and patience? What about instant gratification and self-control? . . . A central virtue of biblical faith is fidelity. Christians aspire to be . . . faithful to one particular God, not to a succession or collection of gods. Likewise, Christian . . . marriage is an exercise in the virtue of fidelity. A Christian marries and commits him- or herself exclusively to a particular mate—"till death do us part."
>
> The consumer, on the other hand, marries because marriage will serve his or her interests, as he or she understands them at the moment. Commitment in the Christian way of life is an ideal and a goal; commitment in the consumer way of life is more . . . typically a temporary good. Marriage in the consumer ethos is too often open to reevaluation. If at any point it fails to promote the self-actualization of one or another spouse, the option of ending the partnership must be available.
>
> In the Christian way, lifetime monogamy makes sense. In the consumer way of life, serial monogamy (a succession of mates, one at a time) is a much more sensible practice. (29)

It is idolatrous to suggest that human fulfillment comes from accumulating more possessions or "possessing" more people. Sexual conquests are admired. Sex appeal sells everything from toothpaste to automobiles. Recently, a cancer-detection ad on the back of a Christian magazine headlined, "Before you read this, take your clothes off." Then in fine print, it counseled how to do bodily self-examinations. (25)

In *Love and Living,* Thomas Merton writes about "Love and Need: Is Love a Package or a Message?"

Love is regarded as a deal. . . . We come to consider ourselves and others not as persons but as products—as "goods," or in other words, as packages. . . . Life is more interesting when you make a lot of deals with a lot of new customers. . . . We are biological machines endowed with certain urges that require fulfillment. If we are smart, we can exploit and manipulate these urges in ourselves and in others. We can turn them to our own advantage. We can cash in on them, using them to satisfy and enrich our own ego by profitable deals with other egos. (29)

The casualties of consumerism include simple living, deferring immediate gratification for the sake of long-term goals, patience, generosity to others, modesty, restraint and self-discipline, and wholesome male-female friendships.

We Western Christians cannot escape the consumer culture. Even though it is counter to our values, to a great extent we have bought into it. Nevertheless, we can and must resist it. This resistance must be a joint effort between both young people and adults. Young people are not likely to defy the culture of their peers until their parents and mentors exhibit some conscientious objection to the consumerist system.

Individualism

Consumerism and individualism go hand in hand. The individualist insists, "What I do, where I go, who I associate with, and what I acquire—these are my business and mine alone." This attitude is not new. In the Old Testament book of Judges two identical verses describe a period of disorder: "In those days there was no king in Israel; all the people did what was right in their own eyes" (17:6; 21:25; NRSV), as they "saw fit." In Proverbs 21:2 we read, "All deeds are right in the sight of the doer, but the Lord weighs the heart" (NRSV).

The apostle Paul begins Romans 14 with instructions against judging one another. He writes about being tolerant of those with differing opinions and those who are at different stages of maturity. Then he says, "We do not live to ourselves, and we do not die to ourselves" (14:7, NRSV). How true.

Christians are all a part of a body. We are a community that looks out for one another. We should be ready to curb our interests for the sake of the community. What I do in private, in my home, in my bedroom, in my sexual behavior—that is, in a real way, not just my business. Each of us is a contributing member of our collective witness. Even our private acts are building or tearing down a community.

In a myriad subtle ways, each private life and behavior collectively creates the pattern of habits, attitudes, and behaviors that tell the world around us, "This is how it is done here, in this community, in this family." Like it or not, we do not and cannot live in total privacy. Our private behavior does influence our public witness.

The health of a community, especially a faith community, depends in part on the health of the sexual relationships within it. So we in faith communities have much sexual agenda with which to deal.

Secularism

The religious, moral voice has been muted in the public square. United States society, established with separation of church and state, has evolved into one where the religious voice is often ignored or even not tolerated, as we note from repeated court and school board decisions. Part of it is the fault of the churches themselves. We have been so contentious over the years, so intolerant of each other's views, and so sectarian and divisive. The courts and government bodies maintain that religious convictions have to contend with all other forces in trying to influence public policy. Even with first-amendment rights, Christians often feel they cannot be effectively heard.

Politicians do profess faith and woo blocks of religious people. Yet in large measure, religion has become privatized. In *Christian Century,* Martin E. Marty reflects this idea:

> Assemble mixed company. Make any assertion you'd like
> about the pope, one or another side of the Southern Baptist
> Convention, Mormons, Christian Scientists, Jews, the Nation
> of Islam, Jesus, Joseph, and Mary. Then listen to the fights
> you've started between the religious. You can't blame politi-
> cians, textbook writers, or playwrights like Suzanne Hannon
> for avoiding all subjects that get close to religion. Hence, a
> culture of disbelief. Hence, a secular society. (879)

We Christians thus bear some of the responsibility for taking God, except for a few hints of religious history, out of the textbooks, and for removing references to religion or church from children's television. Especially is that voice missed when the subject is sex. Here we have a wonderful gift (sexuality) given by God to all members of the human family, and yet the religious voice is silenced. Without the religious, moral voice dominating the discussion of sexual values and mores, should we be surprised that our society has assumed the sexual character it has?

Dualism

Dualism is the persistent notion that we can separate spirit and body. Although in recent years the church has made long strides in viewing people as whole beings, dualism still rears its head. We have made great progress in viewing our sexuality in positive ways, as a wonderful gift from God, yet sexual sins are still considered to be worse than any other. The term *immorality* is used much less often in connection with destructive business practices than it is in referring to negative sexual practices.

We still have some fear of our bodies, especially our sexual bodies, as being dangerous. We think, "My body may cause me to sin." Especially from men, we still hear the same old excuses: "Well, I couldn't help it. I had this overwhelming urge, this uncontrollable passion. It's not my fault. He or she tempted me beyond my human capacity to resist."

When we engage in some illicit sexual behavior, we do not leave our souls parked outside in the driveway. What my body does is "all of me" doing it. I am a whole person. I am fully accountable for my body's activity. I am spirit, mind, and body. I am responsible for all of my behavior. The body does not run on automatic pilot.

Some studies have shown that regular church attendance and an increased level of religious devotion result in reduced rates of extramarital sex and sexually transmitted diseases among young people. But even so, the rates of these are too high among Christian young people.

Dr. C. Everett Koop, former surgeon general of the United States, believes that teenagers will develop strong Christian standards only when Christian parents teach their children early and appropriately about sexuality, sexual behavior, and the moral, ethical, and religious reasons governing it.

Body, mind, and spirit are interconnected and interdependent, and each influences the others. Because of this, we can avoid the dualistic understanding of who we are as sexual beings and be the whole people we are meant to be.

Idolatry

Our society has made sexual fulfillment (as the world defines it) an idol. Sexual intercourse has become the marker for human happiness. Sexual activity without commitment, without covenant, is the standard. We have also made an idol of physical beauty, and we disregard the quality of the person. When people, particularly females, try to meet an unrealistic standard of "beauty" set by a sex-crazed culture, there are long-term negative effects. This can be extremely damaging to one's self-concept.

One aspect of the idolatry is the worship of "sexual freedom"—but it is not freedom. True sexual freedom is realized best within a committed covenantal, exclusive relationship, where we can enjoy the freedom to be ourselves:

- To not be on trial
- To not have to perform
- To not be compared with previous partners
- To learn together
- To trust that my beloved is fully committed to me alone
- To say no as well as yes
- To laugh at ourselves

Such experiences compose true sexual freedom. In *The Search for Intimacy*, Elaine Storkey says so much of the sexual activity in our society takes place under conditions that exclude intimacy. Examples are rape, multiple sexual encounters, adultery, and pornography. These violate the spirit of intimacy. She challenges the church to "help re-establish the wonderful humanness of sex" (190).

Too many turn to this idol—sex, coitus, sexiness, casual coupling—to fill the void in their lives. Yet they end up with their real need still unmet and only greater loneliness and fractured feelings to show for it. Our society's sexual preoccupation is a false god, an idol, and it distorts our understanding of who we are, who God is, and the purposes for which we were created. Living our sexuality in accord with God's purposes for sexual union is the only way to find real joy and true sexual fulfillment. That purpose for sexual union is spelled out in the New Testament, where sexual union (sexual intercourse) is placed firmly within the context of marriage.

Consumerism, individualism, secularism, dualism, and idolatry—we must reckon with these five characteristics of our society in exploring our sexual understandings and mores today. We can test our behavior by asking, "What works?" The consumerist, individualist, secular, dualist, and idolatrous behaviors of our genitally focused society that we see around us are not working. We see altogether too many losers. Later in this chapter we will return to the question "What works?"

Identifying these five traits of our society can give insight on how our culture spawns attitudes that permit—

- language that ignores or insults at least half of the human race.
- suggestive remarks, off-color jokes, and actions that make persons to whom they are directed feel uncomfortable and devalued.
- the production, sale, and purchase of photos, print materials, films, videos, and computer software meant to be a sexual turn-on, that exploit and objectify the bodies of both men and women, but especially women.
- relating to others from unequal power bases and coercing others to "do as I say."
- seeking instant sexual gratification regardless of its effect on ourselves or others.
- breaking commitments, and thus destroying the trust of others.

Let us look at the destructive nature and effects of such behaviors and recognize that all people have had some experience in each of these areas and are in need of forgiveness in relation to them.

Exclusive Language

Consciousness has been raised in recent years, in some settings, to use pronouns in speech, writing, and song that include both women and men in the messages sent. The use of masculine pronouns to represent the whole human race is insensitive to women and no longer acceptable among people who recognize the pain of exclusion. Christian people have an obligation to use the most sensitive manner possible in helping educate others who have not recognized this pain. Modeling the use of inclusive language may be the most effective educational approach. Use of exclusive language has a long history and will take time to change. We are making progress.

Sexual Harassment

Where does good fun and harmless teasing cross the fine line to become sexual harassment? This is not an easy question to answer because the particular circumstances are crucial in deciding. In addition, our sense of what constitutes harassment differs. However, in another sense, the question is not that hard to answer. In making this decision, start by respecting the golden rule: "In everything, do to others what you would have them do to you" (Matt. 7:12).

Answering some pertinent questions can help to guide our behavior: Does this comment or action foster or damage self-esteem in the other person? Does it respect the person's character or exploit the person's body? Is the speaker or actor thinking or caring about how these words or actions might affect the other person or only considering how he or she is portraying himself or herself among like-minded peers? Is this a loving thing to do or say?

Some men say, "I never would have been offended by what I said to her, but she surely was." Are men and women coming from such different places and life experiences that we really cannot predict how persons of the other sex will respond to the same stimuli? To some extent, yes. However, it is important to learn to be sensitive enough to read the body language of another person.

When a person becomes uncomfortable, that person inevitably give cues that indicate this. I have been known to develop a creeping blush from my upper chest to my neck and face. Some will just become silent, lose eye contact, or move away from the setting. Others engage in useless movements of their hands and bodies, sometimes called fidgeting. We have all seen people who get teary-eyed when embarrassed. Some assertive types will begin a loud, accusatory, verbal barrage in response to offensive treatment.

It is much more effective and educational not to attack but to state clearly, "I do not appreciate being spoken to or touched in that way. Please do not do that anymore." This communicates clearly that I have a problem with what has just occurred. Whether or not it seems like a problem to the perpetrator of the harassment, it is not acceptable to me. This allows me to own the problem and not accuse the other of being a bad person.

If that approach is not effective in stopping the assault, further steps can be taken such as keeping a record of specific harassment experiences (who, where, what, when, and who witnessed them), bringing the problem to the attention of people in positions of authority, and using existing channels or help to establish ways of dealing with these infractions.

Sometimes we contribute to sexual harassment by means other than speaking or doing. Laughing at raunchy jokes; giving a thumbs-up or thumbs-down expression as an evaluation of someone's body; posting on our walls seductive pictures that objectify the people portrayed; playing and listening to suggestive music; or spending hours with pornographic materials in print, film, or the Internet—these all contribute to becoming part of the problem and not a part of the solution.

Pornography

It is estimated that pornography in the United States is an eight-to-ten-billion-dollar-a-year business (Pellauer: 345). One of the new venues for producing and utilizing pornography is found in computer software. A program currently being pilot-tested has this as a part of its promotional advertising:

> You can watch them [the virtual girlfriend and boyfriend], talk to them, ask them questions, tell them secrets, and relate with them. Watch them as you ask them to take off different clothes and guide them through many different activities. Watch and participate in the hottest sexual activities available on computer, including: several sexual positions, using many unique toys, even bringing in multiple partners. . . . They will remember your name, birthday, your likes, and your dislikes. Every time you start the program, they say different things and act differently. Each time they have a different personality. (C & M Promotions)

All of us, being human and therefore sexual, find this kind of imagery sexually titillating, and we may be tempted to search for it. Once involved, some people find themselves becoming addicted and needing to spend more and more time with pornographic materials to fulfill their sexual appetites—never getting enough.

Sexually stimulating material is not always pornographic. There often is confusion about the distinction between pornography and erotica. Pornographic materials portray degradation, humiliation, objectification, exploitation, and often violence and aggression toward others. Erotica is material that reflects the spirit of love known as *eros*.

James B. Nelson, a widely published Christian sexual ethicist, says that *eros* (from which the word *erotic* is derived) is one of many words the Greeks had for love. "It is that part of human loving that is born of desire and hunger. Eros feeds me, fills me, makes me more alive." He reminds us that we are bodily people and as such we are "hungry all the time—born to be erotic" (1997 lecture).

Erotica is sexually stimulating material, but in a positive

context. In erotic presentations, "sex is portrayed as part of the broad spectrum of human emotions present in intimate relationships. The people involved are shown to be complex human beings with a variety of nonsexual feelings in addition to sexual ones. . . . Erotica reflects a balance of mutual respect, affection, and pleasure" (Kelly: 445).

When misused,

> the erotic . . . has been made into the confused, the trivial, the psychotic, the plasticized sensation. For this reason, we have often turned away from the exploration and consideration of the erotic as a source of power and information, confusing it with its opposite, the pornographic. But pornography is a direct denial of the power of the erotic, for it represents the suppression of true feeling. Pornography emphasizes sensation without feeling. (Lorde: 76)

There remains some ambiguity about the role of erotica in the lives of sexually healthy Christian people. We do get some help in determining this in a general way from Scripture: Paul says, "Live by the Spirit, and you will not gratify the desires of the sinful nature. . . . The fruit of the Spirit is love, joy, peace, patience, kindness, goodness, faithfulness, gentleness, and self-control" (Gal. 5:16, 22-23). Enjoying bodily pleasures is certainly part of what it means to be human. The ability to control those appetites is also a part of what is expected of human beings created in God's image.

Eroticism is in stark contrast to pornography. Our college sexuality classes learn about how some pornographers go to extremes of exploitation to sexually stimulate others, or more accurately, to sell their products. The students often become incensed that society allows these people to be so highly rewarded for their despicable acts. One wrote in her journal, "Women are made to feel like a piece of meat—nothing more!" Another said, "The limit for me comes when children are portrayed in sexually seductive ways to satisfy adult sexual cravings."

Christians must be alert to the insidious evil of pornography that is permeating the minds of so many people. Now it is even being brought into Christian homes through the Internet.

Countering this kind of multibillion-dollar enterprise will demand constant vigilance and effort on the part of all Christians. We need to help young as well as older people avoid being seduced into a lifestyle that makes room for such garbage. It is gratifying to see that on our Christian campuses so many students, once they are informed, are moved to consider taking action and speaking out against pornography in their local communities. This is a job for every Christian.

Sexual Coercion

When sexual decisions are made from unequal power bases, coercion is likely to result. It may be overt, as in the case of sexual abuse and rape; or it may be subtle, as when sexual favors are an unspoken expectation after someone has spent a significant amount of money to entertain another. These examples reflect the power-holder's self-centeredness and lack of respect for the other person.

The negative things that result when sex is forced on another against that person's will are well-known to those who have survived such events:

- The victims question their personal worthiness.
- They feel that somehow they themselves brought about the event.
- They have a feeling of personal violation.
- They lose their sense of what constitutes appropriate boundaries.
- They lack interest in taking care of their physical body and appearance.
- They tend to drift toward sexual promiscuousness.
- The victims cannot view their sexuality in a wholesome way or relate to a loving, caring spouse in a healthy,

spontaneous, and unencumbered way.

These and many more negative results have been well documented in numerous studies and personal stories.

Alcohol is often involved when sexual abuse and rapes occur. Our local newspaper recently reported that a twenty-one-year-old woman in our community was raped early Sunday morning. She said she had been out drinking on Saturday night. Shortly after returning home, two male "friends" came over. They also allegedly had been drinking. One of the men helped her make it upstairs to her room. She says she does not remember anything else until she realized one of the men was having sex with her. The second man then also had sex with her. She says she was too intoxicated to say no or to resist.

Such illustrations cause many Christians to dismiss the problems as belonging to other people—not me and my acquaintances. Statistics, however, show that battering, incest, and other abuses occur almost as frequently in Christian homes as in the general population. This is difficult to comprehend.

It is a long, complex, and difficult process to try to help persons involved in coercive sexual activities, either as perpetrators or as victims. This is important work that must be done in the most sensitive way possible. It is also urgent to support efforts to prevent sexual coercion. This is where the Christian community should have much to offer through example, education, and the presentation of God's way as a better option.

Instant Sexual Gratification

Unwillingness to control our sexual urges and delay sexual gratification leads to major problems in our society. Here we give attention to two of these issues.

Adolescent Pregnancy and Parenting

Not the least of these major problems is adolescent pregnancy and parenting.

Each year, nearly one million teenagers in the United States—approximately 10 percent of all 15- to 19-year-old females—become pregnant. About one-third of these teens abort their pregnancies, 14 percent miscarry, and 52 percent (or more than half a million teens) bear children, 72 percent of them out of wedlock. . . . More than 175,000 of these new mothers are 17 years old or younger. . . . More than 80 percent of these young mothers end up in poverty. (Maynard: 1).

The fathers of these babies tend to be an average of two and a half years older than the mothers; in one-fifth of the cases, they are at least six years older (Alan Guttmacher Institute, 1994). The long-term effects of early reproduction are extensive and generally negative.

The odds are stacked against the offspring of adolescent mothers from the moment they enter the world. As they grow, they are more likely than children of later childbearers to have health and cognitive disadvantages and to be neglected or abused. The daughters of adolescent mothers are more likely to become adolescent moms themselves, and the sons are more likely to wind up in prison. (Maynard: 5)

The adolescent mother has "a 50 percent lower likelihood of completing high school, 24 percent more children, and 57 percent more time as a single parent during the first 13 years of parenthood" (Maynard: 12). The Robin Hood Study found that the consequences of adolescent childbearing on both younger and older fathers are not as sharp as the effects on mothers and their children. Yet there were some impacts, especially on younger dads, such as not completing high school and having less earning capacity.

People at every age have a series of developmental tasks to accomplish. For the adolescent, these include the developmental tasks of establishing personal identity, separating from parents, considering educational and vocational interests, establishing effective social relationships with peers, and establishing personal values and a workable philosophy of life.

When a pregnancy occurs, the adolescent female's focus necessarily moves from her personal identity to consideration of the new life forming within her. At the very time when it is important to gain distance from her parents, she is forced to become even more dependent upon them and their emotional and financial support. Plans for further education and vocational preparation and involvement are often thwarted due to lack of funds and/or childcare needs.

At the time when peers mean everything, a pregnant adolescent or teen parent often is not able to hang out with the crowd. The young parent needs to assume adult responsibilities before being ready or capable of handling them. This often fosters confusion, frustration, anxiety, and anger in them. Life's script is interrupted and most likely changed forever. "What do I value?" "What is the meaning of my life?" These are questions plaguing pregnant teens even though they may not be able to verbalize them.

Some women and men who find themselves facing parenthood at a young age are blessed to have loving support from family, friends, church, and/or community resources. The experience will most likely be a maturing influence in their lives. It need not be a negative entrapment, even though this seems to happen for many.

The male sexual partner of the pregnant teen may or may not assume responsibility or offer financial or emotional support to his pregnant partner. Sometimes he goes on with his life as though nothing significant has happened, ignoring the needs of his partner and baby. Many males will try to become involved in caring for the mother and child, but they may or may not be in a position to be very helpful. Lack of employment, education, or long-term interest may militate against his being positively involved. Marriage may not be a good option when the couple is immature.

When God's way is chosen, people do not need to deal with these negative consequences of adolescent pregnancy. Then the couple delays sexual intercourse until marriage and makes a long-term commitment to each other. Currently, there is hope that the rate of premarital sex among teenagers in the United States has peaked. A recently released government survey shows a 5 percent decline in the total of unmarried teens of both sexes, between the ages of 15 and 19, who say they have had sexual intercourse. The trend had been steadily increasing since the 1970s (Wallace: 1997).

The Christian community can again be instrumental in upholding the better way for young people. But when youth decide to be sexually active before marriage, they are especially in need of a loving, caring community that will provide support of their personhood and worth and will not be judgmental of their actions. In this situation, we need to follow Jesus' example: he loved those whom society spurned and considered sinners.

Sexually Transmitted Diseases

Another sexuality-related problem of epidemic proportions in our society, one which comes from having sexual intercourse with infected and multiple partners, is that of sexually transmitted diseases.

> An estimated 12 million new sexually transmitted infections occur annually in the United States; two-thirds are among people under the age of 25. At current rates, at least one American in four will acquire a sexually transmitted disease (STD) at some point in his or her life. . . . As many as 56 million Americans may be infected with an incurable viral infection *other than* human immunodeficiency virus (HIV), which causes AIDS. (Alan Guttmacher Institute: 1)

In addition to some STDs being life threatening, they can lead to infertility, ectopic pregnancy, cancer, chronic liver disease, and recurrent or chronic pain. Women, teenagers, and minorities suffer disproportionately from STDs, and the financial burdens exceed five billion dollars annually in the United States.

With these kinds of statistics, Christian parents can justifiably be concerned that there will be a limited number of disease-free persons available for their young adult children to marry. As far as exposure to STDs is concerned, when two people have sexual intercourse, they are really having sexual relations with every person with whom their partners have ever had intercourse. STDs are just that—more than twenty different diseases that are sexually transmitted. The more partners one has had, the greater the risks of contracting one or more STDs.

When STDs are preventable, why do people opt for sexual behavior that brings this kind of physical and emotional risk? The reasons certainly are complex. Nevertheless, young people typically think they are immune: "It can't happen to me."

It is important for God's people to clearly communicate again that God's way is the best way. If everyone committed himself or herself to one sexual partner for life, the scourge of STDs would end. When a person already has had more than one sexual partner, it is appropriate to begin now to hold to this standard of becoming monogamous.

Broken Commitments

As noted in the earlier chapter on intimacy, one of the important ingredients of a truly intimate relationship is trust. Trusting another person means that we believe that person will keep promises made. We feel secure in knowing that commitments made are taken seriously and upheld. We know that a person in whom we trust will have our best interests in mind and will use good judgment about divulging anything about us to others. When someone breaks those commitments and promises, the partner experiences a devastating loss of trust. The betrayed partner may never again perceive the other to be quite as reliable even though confession and forgiveness may have occurred.

In our society, commitments made in marriage vows are often broken through adultery and divorce. There are many reasons for the destruction of marriages.

> Most of those who research the divorce epidemic note that a key cause is over-inflated expectations of emotional bliss and romantic love. . . . While Christians can do all that lies within our power to nurture happy, loving, and joyful marriages, at the same time we must assert that in God's plan, people are not free to go from one marriage to the next, looking for greater bliss. (Gushee: 19)

It is surprising to note that only 20 percent of divorces are caused by an affair, according to John Gottman, a professor of psychology at the University of Washington in Seattle. "Most marriages die with a whimper, as people turn away from one another, slowly growing apart" (1997). The mundane events of everyday life build or damage love in marriage. Our way of relating in the countless "mindless moments" that usually go by unnoticed establishes a positive or negative emotional climate.

This growing apart is usually not anticipated. Marriage partners may begin to give increasing attention to appropriate endeavors—so much so that the marriage relationship is neglected. "A career can be the third party in marital infidelity. Too often a marriage is destroyed because one spouse has unwittingly married the children and the other spouse has married a career" (Hunt and Hunt: 76).

Conflicting values also may contribute to the destruction of marriages. Couples are often caught between

> the value of lifelong marriage covenant and commitment to stable families on the one hand, and on the other the value of individual freedom which says each person, male and female, ought to be free to pursue their own dreams, gifts, ca-

reer. Both American culture and the Christian church are
searching for a balance between these two conflicting loyalties. (Sider and Sider: 38)

When faced with this conflict, even the church too often set-
tles for an either/or approach. "Legitimate individual fulfillment need not be sacrificed on the altar of 'family values'; nor
does the nurture and care of children need to be sacrificed on
the altar of selfish individualism" (Sider and Sider: 38). There
is a need for

> Christian marriages where both partners seek to nurture the
> other's joy and personal fulfillment, practicing mutual sub-
> mission. Patriarchy does not work. Self-centered feminism—
> and its counterpart, self-centered male irresponsibility—does
> not work. Mutual submission, practiced over a lifetime of
> joy, pain, struggle, and growth, is just what our hurting
> homes need. (Sider and Sider: 38)

What works? God's design for our lives works. It is the only
design that lives up to its promise. Only God's design can bring
us real joy, true intimacy, and true sexual fulfillment. What has
been described in this chapter are five components of the mold
into which the world tries to press us and some of the result-
ing behaviors from these influences.

Paul says, "Don't let it happen." Refuse to be perpetually dissatisfied, always wanting more. Refuse to settle for that which
yields only temporary pleasure. Refuse to be silent in the public arena. Refuse to make sex our idol. Refuse to remain self-
centered. We can and must give *nonconformity* new life, new
meaning, and new urgency. We can and must create in our
faith communities a sexual counterculture, better than that of
the world. With God's help we can do it. This is at least part
of what Paul is telling us to do in Romans 12:2.

A passage from 1 John 2:15-17 gives us guidance:

Stop loving this evil world and all that it offers you, for when you love these things you show that you do not really love God; for all these worldly things, these evil desires—the craze for sex, the ambition to buy everything that appeals to you, and the pride that comes from wealth and importance— these are not from God. . . . This world is fading away, and these evil, forbidden things will go with it, but whoever keeps doing the will of God will live forever. (TLB)

When we look for the culprits that have led to the kinds of damaging sexuality-related behaviors described in this chapter, look behind the pornographers, the actors, the TV moguls, the advertisers, and the MTV producers. Behind all of these, we find ourselves, who have allowed the world to press us into its mold. We are in need of transformation, declares Paul in Romans 12:2. Nonconformity is a concept that must be reaffirmed in our generation and in a more-relevant and urgent form than ever before. As God's children, we *can* experience the goodness of the gift of sexuality as we were meant to do.

Discussion Questions

1. Is the development of a sexual counterculture possible? Where might individuals and congregations begin this development?
2. How might Christian people reinstate a religious and moral voice in discussions of sexual values and mores in our society?
3. How are individuals' private sexual behaviors impacting your community—toward or away from health?
4. If you are reading these questions in a group setting, determine if the members of the group have different or similar ideas about what constitutes sexual harassment.
5. How might congregations respond to the issue of pornography?

6. Now that consciousness has been raised in various sources about the prevalence of sexual abuse in "Christian" homes, how should Christians respond?
7. What steps might individuals, families, and congregations take in trying to prevent the occurrence of adolescent pregnancy and sexually transmitted diseases in the community?

12

The Gift Restored

Delores Histand Friesen

THERE ARE no easy ways to describe how restoration, healing, therapy, and forgiveness take place. Previous chapters have detailed some of the many ways we can misuse, ignore, or destroy the gifts of sexuality, integrity, and intimacy.

We cannot reduce the healing process to techniques or advice or scriptural guidelines. Recovery is first a *process*: it takes time to experience restoration and healing. It comes as God's power, and the love and safety of the community help to cleanse and restore the identity and integrity of the person. Because our sexuality is relational, it requires human connection, communication, and dialogue.

Instead of giving general guidelines for persons who have experienced disappointment, victimization, or harassment, this chapter is directed toward the church. More specifically, it will promote a biblical and life-affirming view of the gift of sexuality. Such a view will help to provide a healing climate and resources for healing and restoration. This chapter deals with the congregation's role in restoring the gift of sexuality. Yet individuals and families who are seeking healing will also find ways to take steps toward healing.

After I clarify that we need to give more attention to sexuality in our lives and ministries, I will give practical suggestions on climate, community, caregiving, and confrontation. Then I will present some goals and principles that every congregation would do well to implement.

I encourage persons facing problems, concerns, and hurts in the area of sexuality to reach out to others who can be trusted. They may share their stories with those in their circle of friends and their congregation who are best able to understand, listen, and walk with them through the process of healing. Inviting others to a "meeting for clearness" or sharing the healing power of liturgical dance and the expressive arts, for example, can bring restoration to both the individuals and the congregation.

Climate

A climate of safety and acceptance is one of the first things that makes it possible for persons to share their experiences, hurts, and needs. Listening needs to come from both the heart and the head. Parker J. Palmer names some qualities that are helpful in establishing a healing climate where persons can risk exposing their hurts, failures, and desires. These include respect; structure or intentionality; accountability; the ability to listen carefully, not only to what is said, but also to what is left unsaid; and a willingness to take risks (69, 74).

Palmer describes six paradoxical tensions that create a hospitable space where learning and growth can take place:
- The space should be bounded and open.
- The space should be hospitable and "charged."
- The space should invite the voice of the individual and the voice of the group.
- The space should honor the "little" stories of the individuals and the "big" stories of the disciplines and tradition.
- The space should support solitude and surround it with the resources of community.
- The space should welcome both silence and speech.

Some years ago on a rainy night, a woman was driving around, wrestling over whether to abort her pregnancy. She saw a sign to a Mennonite church and determined that night to go there and talk to someone before she made the final decision. Today she is a member of that church, and her children have grown up in a place where their voices were and are heard.

Congregations that want to restore persons to wholeness need to consider the climate, openness, and safety of both their physical and spiritual space.

Centrality of Sexuality

A second way for the church to work at restoring the gift of sexuality is to recognize that our sexuality is central to who we are as human beings. Therefore, every congregation and denomination should give attention to sexual issues and education as part of an ongoing process rather than only as a response to crisis or situations of church discipline for sexual sins.

> Legend has it that Carl Jung once remarked that when people brought sexual questions to him, they invariably turned out to be religious questions, and when they brought religious questions, they always turned out to be sexual ones. . . . Inquiry about sexuality almost always has an inevitable religious dimension, . . . not only teachings about sexual morality; [religion] also bears great themes of sexual relevance: . . . creation and God's purpose in creating us as sexual beings, what we believe about human nature and destiny, sin and salvation, love and justice, and community—all these and many other basic beliefs will condition and shape our sexual self-understandings (Nelson: 14).

To restore the gift of sexuality, the church needs to help its people take responsibility for sexual feelings, acts, behaviors, and attitudes. This is best achieved by teaching and preaching forthrightly and clearly about the beauty, joy, and sanctity of sexual expressions both within and outside the conjugal bond. If God created male and female in his image and expected them to relate in intimate, procreative, and relational ways, then this *very good* creation needs to be celebrated and cared for responsibly and joyfully.

In my classes at Mennonite Brethren Biblical Seminary, I ask everyone to prepare a sermon on some aspect of sexuality. There are still too many who look at me incredulously, unable to imagine themselves or their church doing such overt teaching and preaching. Furthermore, some think there is hardly enough biblical material to provide useful texts, except for wedding sermons.

What, I ask them, is the grace of the gospel for those who do not marry? And *when* is such teaching needed? And *how many* wedding services have you attended where any open teaching was given on the sexual aspects of married life?

A survey of Scripture texts found in *Human Sexuality in the Christian Life* shows that the topic appears in more than half of the books in the Bible. If we add the stories of the Bible to the teachings, letters, prophecies, and poetry, there are plenty of significant materials for teaching and preaching.

At least once a year, every congregation should emphasize right relationships and interrelationships between men and women, boys and girls. Many have made a good start by taking one month each year, perhaps February or May, to focus on friendships, fellowship, home, and family concerns. I caution, however, that often the singles, comprising 30 to 40 percent of most average congregations, are woefully neglected in this programming.

In addition to preaching and adult education, congregations should implement a planned age-graded program of sex education. Thereby everyone, from preschooler to those past eighty, is included in the discussion, dialogue, training, and caregiving. The Presbyterian Church USA and United Church of Christ have produced material for such programs.

If this kind of program is carefully followed year after year, it will help to develop healthy attitudes and knowledge of how to talk to one another about sexual matters in appropriate ways. It will create networks of accountability and pastoral care that provide the basis for the healing and processing of the more painful and abusive experiences.

The media and the advertising commercialism of our hedonistic age tend to define social standards. In addition to congregational teaching, preaching, and education, our society needs the church's prophetic ministry.

Advocacy is also sorely needed, not only for victims, but also for the young, the old, the disenfranchised, the disabled, and those newly bereaved. We need some central theological constructs that include justice making, process, and healing. The process of restoring the gift of sexuality can be long and difficult, but it can deepen and enrich the ministry of the church to its members and to the larger world.

Community

Human sexuality is best understood as God's way of enriching and creating community, not just between male and female, but also in the family and wider social structures. There is a danger that sexuality may become an end in itself instead of opening into the infinitely greater experience of connection and intimacy. Then it becomes a narrowing and limiting factor that undermines community and relationships. Instead, sexuality should be creating bonds of love and unity that build friendship, family, and community.

Some other world religions have tended to swing between the two extremes of orgiastic pleasure or denial, excess or celibacy. We support both celibacy and monogamy, with the commitment to become one flesh in a lifelong union.

We need to keep talking and struggling together to offer truly faithful responses to human sexuality. We need to hear about how women and men are relating well in liberating, life-giving ways. "Faithful responses to human sexuality . . . provide food for the journey in our lives of ministry and in our search for and participation in Christian community" (Eugene: 2). Our human sexuality is a wonderful and liberating resource.

We are called to work, not only for social justice, but also for sexual justice. "Sexual injustice, in many forms and on the basis of various customs and mores, is a global sore festering in fear, cruelty, and violence. . . . Patterns of sexual and gender injustice are linked inextricably to those of racial, economic, and other structures of wrong relation" (Eugene: 3).

Sometimes the congregation gives so much emphasis to the devastation of sexual abuse that it ignores those who experience miscarriage, infertility, postpartum depression, impotence, or other sexual difficulties. A young father wrote a thesis about how the church might acknowledge the pain and minister to families who experience miscarriage. He was deeply hurt by the callous way others dealt with the prenatal losses in his own family.

In his work as a minister, he has determined to reach out to men and women with unspoken and unnoticed griefs and longings. This, however, demands and assumes that there is a sense of community and a willingness to open up and share our hurts, questions, fears, and failures with each other.

Restoring the gift may mean that we need to consciously consider who is relating to whom in our congregations. We can work at breaking through the walls of isolation and individualism so easily set up by our modern life. I think, for example, of a young mother of three, isolated on a cold prairie farm. She spent days alone with the children, wondering if she could get through another day without harming one of the children or herself.

When she and her anxious husband poured out their story to me (a safe visitor from outside their community), they were surprised to learn how common postpartum depression is. They were willing to take some steps to seek help and break her isolation and desperation. But it took great courage and a willingness to let others in the congregation know and share their fearful secret.

Others often overlooked include the elderly. Many are living alone. Some formerly married are now single. Seniors may

178 Sexuality: God's Gift

struggle with feelings of inadequacy. Some are disabled or have a chronic illness. Many cannot remember the last time they were hugged. All of us long for the blessing of human touch and compassion. The church has a significant ministry in reaching out to the elderly.

A young teenaged birth mother handed her child in the baptismal font to a Mennonite pastor couple for adoption. As one mother passed the baby through the water to the other mother, words of commitment, release, and joy were shared; tears of sorrow, grief, and connection were shed. This was not a private ceremony. Family members and friends of the teenager were present, as well as church members and friends of the pastor couple. The individual pain and commitment became corporate as they wept with those who wept and rejoiced with those who rejoiced.

It was not easy for the adoptive family and the birth mother to establish a relationship. It will take much wisdom and work for them to maintain appropriate connection and distance. Yet here was a gathered community of God's grace that recognized pain and bonding. They blessed it with a service of release and acceptance, of letting go and holding on. This ceremony of blessing would not have had the same strengthening effect if it had been done in private. Here we see a godly response to circumstances of sexuality. It is also an example of God building community and of working together for good, even through our brokenness and pain.

The previous chapter on broken commitments described consumerism, secularism, dualism, idolatry, exclusive language, sexual harassment, pornography, sexual coercion, and instant sexual gratification. All of these destroy community. Restored sexuality and community begin by first demonstrating the power of loving relationships and then teaching the same. Through our words and actions, we can develop relationships where love, honesty, intimacy, forgiveness, and grace are central and pure.

Caregiving and Confronting

In caregiving and confronting, we work out strategic, practical, and theological responses to a variety of sexuality challenges and issues. We also allow for personal issues to surface and to be dealt with. According to Toinette Eugene,

> The vast majority of religious statements on sexuality in the past have assumed essentially a one-way question, a question posed from a dominant, normative perspective: "What does Christian theology, or the Bible, or the church's tradition say about human sexuality?" . . . [We must also ask,] "What does our experience as sexual human beings say about the ways in which we experience God, interpret our religious tradition, and attempt to live the life of faith?" (2)

A congregation with skilled caregivers has eagerness and enthusiasm to address sexuality issues openly and move toward health, justice, and wholeness. Caregivers act with compassion, to prevent deficits and promote assets. The pastoral issues grow out of ministry experience and involve education within churches, pastoral counseling, and social advocacy. Caregivers provide general attention to sexuality and specific attention to sexual violence and abuse, boundary violations, and sexual deviations and aberrations. They give reasons, not just rules.

The church needs to recognize and acknowledge that increased sexual involvement is occurring at earlier ages. In addition, more Christians are tending to accept such activity as moral. According to Charles Shelton, "More and more adolescents view such activity as morally acceptable. . . . Attitudes about sexual morality are currently guided less by rules and regulations and more by the personal commitment and affection that two people are experiencing" (235).

Responding to sexual issues is much more complex than saying a simple black-and-white yes and no. Many factors must be considered: spiritual, physiological, psychological, cultural, and experiential. A discerning church needs to ask, "What are the issues at stake in *your* life?" Then the church must walk closely enough with the person to help discern that and work toward healing covenant and commitment. Caregivers also need to affirm victims-survivors for breaking the silence, affirm that they were not responsible for the offenses, and affirm the survivors' own healing processes.

The community benefits from those who have experience in guiding discourse and deliberation that overcome ignorance and fear. Leaders need to be comfortable, knowledgeable, and effective in biblical work and be prepared for the challenges of sexuality concerns and issues. Then it is possible for a congregation to hold personal experience in creative tension with religious vision and to affirm the importance of sexuality without giving it undue emphasis.

Minimally, a congregation could have an advocacy team or couple in addition to the care-and-share committee, deacons, or pastoral care listening team. Such advocates need good skills and a willingness to educate themselves about the needs of those who have been harassed, abused, victimized. They also need to learn about the needs of persons who are perpetrators.

Those who provide these training-healing opportunities need to be comfortable with their own sexuality, have a healthy view of and mutual respect for the sexuality of others, be able to discuss without judgment, be lighthearted and humorous, and show appropriate openness.

Carolyn Holderread Heggen's book *Sexual Abuse in Christian Homes and Churches* is a great resource for advocates, deacons, and elders. In addition to the basics, it has helpful chapters on perpetrators, education, liturgies of healing, and many illustrative examples. In *Sexual Offending and Restoration*, Mark Yantzi explains new ways to provide hope to those who have been abused, to the abusers, and to their families.

Jesus ministered to the woman taken in adultery (John 8); the woman at the well, who had a series of partners (John 4); and the demon-possessed man, crazy from mental anguish

(Luke 8). His encounters are biblical examples of how the church might confront and restore with compassion and grace.

In the first encounter, Jesus recognizes that all of us have sinned, not only those caught in flagrant affairs. When the others have recognized their own lack of perfection, Jesus looks at the woman and asks where her accusers are. Then he offers freedom from condemnation: "Go now and leave your life of sin" (John 8:11). When the church recognizes its own failures, it is able to meet people where they are and help them find the way to restore a life where sexuality is honored and decent.

When people have long histories of irresponsibility, confusion, and pain, it may take hours and months of earnest conversation and confrontation. Yet the church and the gospel always hold out hope. Holiness and honor are fruits of right relationships with God and each other; they do not come from impossible standards or rules.

We can ask those whose mixed-up sexualities have driven them and others crazy, "What is your name?" With God's power, believers can still cast out the legion of demons (Luke 8:26-39). Fear, mistrust, loss of identity, and emotional and mental illness respond best to solid compassion and safe boundaries.

Clearness

The Quaker tradition has a custom that could help greatly in learning how to restore each other in a spirit of gentleness. Whoever has a question, decision, or problem to sort out may call a "meeting for clearness." The troubled person selects several people, preferably from a wide range to maximize creativity and response. Then the individual presents a written account of the dilemma or issue that needs healing or discernment.

When the group meets, they first listen to the one who asked for the meeting for clearness. That person describes in some detail what has happened, what the situation is, and the questions over which struggle continues. All participants then may respond only by asking questions for clarification; they may not give advice or counsel.

The way ahead becomes clear as the group continues to ask and the person responds. It is amazing how often a clear consensus is reached. If it is not, the group adjourns and meets again. They follow the same procedure. The group works with a new written account of the directions and struggles clarified the last time. This is a wonderful discipline for pastors, parents, and counselors to only ask—not to tell, explain, or give insight.

Compassion and Holistic Healing

The healing and compassionate ministries of the church need to be grounded in the teachings and life of Jesus. Ministry is also enriched by the psalms of lament, the many stories of God's redeeming and creative acts in history, and the thundering messages of the prophets.

Robert Rencken has used a snow-covered volcano as a metaphor to describe some of the results of sexual abuse. The casual observer may think things look normal or even better than normal. Yet the secretive nature of much sexual abuse covers both the behavior and the damage, sometimes for many years. However, the dormant volcano is there, even though snow may be hiding treacherous rocks and holes.

When the volcano does erupt, there is anger and rage, love and hate, fear and guilt, power and weakness, scars, and perhaps a new face on the mountain. Other family members, friends, and communities may also be buried in lava and snow as indirect victims. The anger, rage, and pain may be seen for years after abuse has ceased. The potential for further eruption continues, unpredictable in time, intensity, and cause (2).

One way to look at a more holistic ministry style is to recognize that these paradoxes of feelings and behaviors are part of the normal course of healing. There is often a tension in the church between focusing on the pain and loss, and focusing on the strength and resiliency that many victims exhibit. There are other tensions: We can individualize and polarize—or organize and communalize. We can move toward forgiveness and reconciliation—or move toward accountability and justice making. We can be concerned about moral responsibility—or be concerned about legal liability. We can emphasize present experience, stress historical accomplishments, or work toward fulfilling future dreams.

Many of these tensions can be resolved by agreeing to face and work through them rather than choosing to deny or avoid the tensions. To confront and support all parties, it takes individual courage, a commitment to study and understand their experiences, and a resolve to help others learn from them.

As part of the process, it often is necessary to refer people to therapists, groups, and agencies outside the congregation. However, referral to others does not lessen the congregation's responsibility and importance of the role the congregation can play. It also does not excuse laypersons from educating and enlarging their minds and hearts so they can be better caregivers and friends. While church members are receiving counseling or therapy, they may need pastoral care and support even more than they did before.

As a therapist, I find it quite helpful to have a pastor or a friend of the client who can provide times and places of nurture, prayer, and safety. This gives the client and therapist the courage and ability to go deeper in the cleansing and restoration process. It often is also encouraging if the congregation establishes a fund for counseling to help restore victims.

When the offender and/or victim are part of the congregation, the tensions or paradoxes are even more pronounced. In addition to the distrust, pain, and loss, there is a tendency for the congregation to polarize into two groups: those who see the need for forgiveness and reconciliation at odds with those who call for accountability and justice making. Others will argue over moral responsibility versus legal liability. Some may try to silence the victim rather than expose the perpetrator.

Abuse must be confronted and reported to the proper authorities as required by law. The community must take action to insure safety for all involved, including potential future victims. If the offender is a pastor, mentor, counselor, or spiritual leader, there must be consequences beyond reprimand or transfer. These consequences have to be tailored to each situation.

See the notes for more resources on sexual abuse by church leaders and others: "Pastoral Sexual Abuse," *MCC Conciliation Quarterly,* Fall 1991; Mennonite Central Committee packets, such as *Crossing the Boundary* and *Broken Boundaries*; and materials from the Center for Prevention of Sexual and Domestic Violence in Seattle.

Conscience and Covenant

Why then does the church experience so much difficulty in providing a healthy view of sexuality and a compassionate and effective healing ministry in the area of sexual abuses? When people are frustrated and facing difficulties, this is an opportune time to work toward healing that is holistic, redemptive, and creative. Making covenant with God and each other is central to this process.

Part of maturing in sexuality is coming to understand one's sexual values, attitudes, feelings, and interests as distinct (and perhaps different) from others. Second, we come to assume responsibility for our own sexual self and behaviors (Shelton: 234).

The youth are not the only ones who construct a personal fable with the assumption that they are personally immune from the consequences of irresponsible or unthinking sexual behavior. Many persons believe that the consequences of sexual behavior can happen to others but not to them. We can see recent extensions of this kind of thinking when people do not take precautions to avoid AIDS and HIV-related illness, excuse politicians and other leaders for illicit and extramarital relationships, and use abortion as a birth-control measure.

Congregations need to name the problems they see, hold each other to accountability, and help individuals know that sex is an act of self-disclosure, intimacy, affection, love, interdependence, maintenance, and exchange. Used responsibly and lovingly, it is very good. Used irresponsibly, it can kill, maim, and destroy.

Individuals and congregations need to determine to take some action and work at preventive strategies. They should learn to recognize the signs, symptoms, and results of abusive behavior. They must insist on appropriate consequences.

For this to happen, the church must see that pastors and other trustworthy members are educated to lead in this area. Individual Christians and congregations need to covenant to take both a proactive and a preventive stance. They can develop programs, policies, and liturgies that are truly responsive and led by the Spirit. Sin and injustice need to be dealt with honestly and compassionately. Churches must foster maturity and responsibility in managing our sexuality.

Change Process

Restoring healthy sexuality is a process requiring significant change and growth. However, change is often resisted because it is painful or scary. The world hunger movement has been helpful in describing the *change process* as a four-step model:
- Heighten awareness.
- Mobilize resources.
- Develop models.
- Reorder structures.

This process helps us enlarge the focus of change to include prevention and social action. For example, if there are incidents of pastoral sexual abuse, the congregation may benefit greatly from inviting consultants to study and to help the group work through their trauma and rebuild leadership and family structure. Those who are determined to survive and overcome need support and advocacy.

A congregation needs to follow due-process procedures and conference policies for responding to similar allegations and situations in other churches. The congregation will also need to wrestle with how it relates accountability to forgiveness. It needs to make sure that adequate mechanisms exist for regulating communications and information.

Often there is a premature desire to move on or to suppress painful, unwanted feelings and issues. There might be a tendency to blame the victims for not healing faster, for "holding on too long." A congregation needs to work at all four levels, not just heightening awareness or reordering structure. Then lasting changes can result.

Writing, journaling, and storytelling are good resources for heightening awareness. Somehow, opening the problem, uncovering it, and putting into words what has been secret or feared for so long—these things release and empower the victim. The victim's story can be told and heard. If the victim can access resources and see models or hear stories of how others have changed or healed, those experiences release powerful healing mechanisms of hope and courage.

Corporate action and worship can help to define events as part of who we are, not something to get over. An annual workshop that focuses on confession, remorse, and hope does much to stop the hidden power of secret, cut-off feelings and thoughts. Ward and Wild's *Human Rites* is a resource with liturgies and celebrations for small groups and family settings as well as public worship. As the congregation mobilizes resources and develops models for healing and remembrance, the gift of sexuality can be restored.

Celebration

If sexuality is a gift that is *very good*, then it deserves to be celebrated and enjoyed. While we consider sexuality as celebration, we do not worship it as an ultimate concern, nor make sexuality so holy and extraordinary that it threatens us or dominates our lives. However, neither should one debase this gift by viewing sex, sexuality, and sensuousness as aspects of life that are essentially evil.

The miracle of birth, committed relationships, and beautiful bodies are celebrated by individuals, couples, and families. The church community also has many events and ways to celebrate the gift of sexuality. In addition to the use of drama, liturgy, liturgical and healing dance, intimacy, friendship, and spiritual direction, there are celebrative events and moments to treasure. They restore us and give us hope.

Three key resources for the healing process are often neglected: liturgy, drama, and sacred dance. Some years ago, a young seminarian told me the moving story of how her participation in sacred dance helped her to heal from multiple experiences of physical and sexual abuse.

Her body had been violated by violence, blows, and unwanted sexual contact. Hence, she found it empowering and healing to be able later to use her body as a vehicle for God's grace and love. To flow with abandon in front of a congregation; to lead others in worship; to feel her body expressing the Spirit, the creative acts and love of God, and the compassion of Jesus—these experiences healed her at a far-deeper level and in a more-lasting way than years of therapy, confession, prayer, and confrontation.

In personal and corporate worship, many people find the use of movement to be a powerful symbol of growth, joy, peace, and love. In *Embodied Prayer*, the author suggests selecting a familiar hymn such as "Have Thine Own Way, Lord." Experience it in silence with a friend, one person acting as potter, the other as clay, and then reverse the roles as the song continues to play (Schroeder: 194-195).

Since the sexual act is so dramatic and the consequences of

its misuse are so great, drama can also deeply touch the soul. Years ago, Mennonite Central Committee sponsored a training event on sexual abuse where some people performed an original drama. The silence, the chilling recognition of truth, the helplessness of the characters, the despicableness of the act— all these have remained with me long after the testimonies, speeches, and workshops have faded.

In another conference in British Columbia, the smashing of a crystal vase that held a long-stemmed rose made it abundantly clear that something precious is lost when a person is violated. *From Crescent to Circle: A Survivors' Liturgy for Worship, Grief and Hope*, by Linda Nafziger-Meiser, uses stones, fabric, Scripture, and songs to celebrate and confront the stone of memory and the stone of help. Such worship effectively includes grieving and hoping.

In *A Winter's Song*, Jane Keen allows the participants to select the level of forgiveness with which they feel most comfortable. She encourages victims to acknowledge and choose the gifts of forgiveness and restoration in the ways and times and places they are able to celebrate.

Hope and Vision

Achieving wholeness and restoration involves the work of God's Spirit, but it often takes the conscience and commitment of God's people to stay with the process. How am I or how are we hindering or helping this movement of God in our midst?

The congregation models, teaches, and upholds the vision of forgiveness, restoration, purity, holiness, joy, celebration, unity as one flesh—and the enjoyment of the erotic and the body as in the Song of Songs (Sol.). We count the creation of male and female as *very good* (Gen. 1:26-31). The church continues the creative and redemptive work of God. It offers the love, forgiveness, and compassion of Jesus and the discernment, blessing, and empowerment of the Holy Spirit. These actions build community and break down dividing walls.

I close this chapter with two visions and a request that your congregation's families, agencies, and institutions hold a meeting for clearness. Set some vision and direction for how you might go about the work of God in restoring those who have been hurt and that which has been destroyed. The questions at the end of the chapter may be helpful in this process.

First, let us look at two visions of redemption and restoration. Join in the creative and redemptive work of God; the love, compassion, and forgiveness of Jesus; and the discernment and blessing of the Holy Spirit's empowerment.

Walter and Ingrid Trobisch were a German-American couple who worked as missionaries in Cameroon, West Africa. After hundreds of letters and a series of booklets on questions of love and marriage, they found themselves in demand as speakers and workshop leaders.

One day they were ministering in a West African city and met a confirmed bachelor named Maurice, thirty-eight and still a virgin. He had lived with his mother and valued his privacy and the sanctity and purity of his life. They also met Fatma, a prostitute who had experienced almost every sexual aberration, including abuse, abortion, rape, and attempted suicide. How Maurice and Fatma came together is a miracle story worth reading in *I Married You*.

Fatma declares, "I am an adulteress and a murderess. I killed my baby." She asks, "How can I ever make that good again?" Ingrid puts her arm around her and says, "Fatma, there are things we can never make right again. We can only place them under the cross."

When Maurice remonstrates that this is not the kind of woman he expected or planned to marry, Trobisch replies, "But she is a virgin. . . . She's cleansed—as the bride of Christ. Without spot. Without wrinkle. Without blemish" (Trobisch: 131-135).

The other vision is a visual one that utilizes several senses, including touch and smell. It is a communion box created by a gay man who lives with his partner but still wishes to hold membership in the congregation for which he created this work of art. It is a small box, perhaps eighteen inches square and three inches deep, made of wood, but covered with lamb's wool on the outside. It is lined with red velvet on the inside lid, and with mirrors on the inside walls and bottom of the box.

When the lid of the box is lifted, one is conscious of the sacrifice of the Lamb of God and the shed blood of Jesus, as one experiences the scent of aged wine from the rows of communion glasses carefully placed in the box. The mirrors reflect the red of the velvet. Even more striking is the fact that one's vision is drawn beyond the box and beyond the cups one can touch to the unending rows and lines of communion cups that reach into eternity and infinity.

May the cross of Jesus and the communion of the saints cleanse, equip, and empower each of us for the work of restoration and healing.

Discussion Questions

1. How is the covenantal aspect of sexuality communicated in our congregation, in my home, and in my life?
2. What do I need to communicate to others regarding sexuality?
3. How do my actions or inactions contribute to the building of community or the breakdown of community?
4. What is the climate of my church, family, and neighborhood communities?
5. Where and how might I show compassion? Where do I need healing and restoration?
6. How and when have I (we) celebrated the gift of sexuality? How could I release my gifts and those of others for celebration? (Examples are journaling, writing, singing, dancing, drama, liturgy, prayer.)
7. Should I call or participate in a meeting for clearness?

13

The Gift:
Further Study

*Delores Histand Friesen and
Anne Krabill Hershberger*

EACH TOPIC INCLUDED in this book can be studied to much
greater depth than is possible here. In this chapter, we will list
some of the many resources for further study, in the hope that
readers will be inspired to continue increasing their insights
and understandings of sexuality from the perspectives of many
people. Particular effort has been made to include resources
that represent Christian and Anabaptist perspectives as well as
some secular and scientific resources.

Each resource is listed only once, in a category where it
mostly fits; however, some of the resources could be listed in
many of the categories, due to the wide scope of their contents.
Most of the resources are from the past decade, though some
excellent materials from earlier times could have been listed.

Every resource also has a list of resources used in the production of that document. Use them! One of the most profound biblical concepts regarding the sexual relationship is expressed in the term *knowing*. It is a deep and spiritual experience to truly know oneself and the other person. When we
read, study, and experience other viewpoints, stories, and
questions, we learn to *know* both ourselves and others.

It is hard to read a story like Bell's *My Rose: An African-
American Mother's Story of AIDS* and still ignore the AIDS
issue and the care of persons with AIDS. Watching videos
where survivors of sexual abuse tell their stories increases com-

passion and understanding as well as the urgency to work toward prevention and a safer society. Wrestling with various questions and studies of biblical interpretation stimulates dialogue, understanding, and growth.

Conflicts and disagreements press us to do more study. Like the apostle Paul, Christians need to ask for the parchments and give attention to reading. If you are a congregational leader or teacher, you may wish to plan a yearly study or sermon series on human sexuality, taking one topic at a time. If you are working through family or personal issues or questions, then choose those areas of study and resources that speak to your needs. Above all, do not be afraid to ask questions and search the Scriptures as you study and read. Take time to reflect, pray, and study with other Christian believers.

It is a good discipline to come to resources such as these with an open mind and a teachable spirit. The "meeting for clearness" can take place as you study. Respond by continuing to ask questions as you think rather than arguing or trying to promote your own ideas. Build convictions and engage in actions based on Scripture, community, and dialogue. Using resources such as these is one way to take seriously both the community of faith and the worlds of science, art, and knowledge.

May God's gift of sexuality continue to be a good gift that is treasured, honored, and understood. This is our prayer:

God, you have created us and called us to a life of holiness, joy, and union. May we accept and treasure the goodness and grace of sexuality. Help us to grow in our acceptance of ourselves and each other despite differences in orientation, conviction, and interpretation. Send your Holy Spirit to guide and teach us how to love and be loved. Through Jesus Christ our Lord. Amen.

Adolescent Sexuality and Pregnancy

Carrera, Michael A. *Lessons for Lifeguards: Working with Teens When the Topic Is Hope.* PO Box 20583, New York 10021-0071: Donkey Press, 1996.

Dash, Leon. *When Children Want Children: An Inside Look at the Crisis of Teenage Parenthood.* New York: Penguin Books, 1989.

Howard, M. *How to Help Your Teenager Postpone Sexual Involvement.* New York: Continuum Pub. Co., 1989.

Maynard, Rebecca A., ed. *Kids Having Kids.* New York: Robin Hood Foundation, 1996.

Musick, J., et al. *Young, Poor, and Pregnant: The Psychology of Teenage Pregnancy.* New Haven: Yale Univ. Press, 1993.

Pipher, Mary. *Reviving Ophelia: Saving the Selves of Adolescent Girls.* New York: Ballantine Books, 1994.

Roggow, Linda, and Carolyn Owens. *Pregnant and Single: Help for the Tough Choices.* Scottdale, Pa.: Herald Press, 1998.

Shelton, Charles M. *Adolescent Spirituality: Pastoral Ministry for High School and College Youth.* New York: Crossroads, 1989.

Thompson, Sharon. *Going All the Way: Teenage Girls' Tales of Sex, Romance, and Pregnancy.* New York: Hill and Wang, Div. of Farrer, Straus, and Giroux, 1995.

Voydanoff, P., and B. Donnelly. *Adolescent Sexuality and Pregnancy.* Newbury Park, Calif.: Sage Publications, 1990.

Acquired Immunodeficiency Syndrome (AIDS)

Amos, William E., Jr. *When AIDS Comes to Church.* Louisville: Westminster, 1998.

Bell, Geneva E. *My Rose: An African-American Mother's Story of AIDS.* Cleveland: Pilgrim Press, 1997.

Bender, David L., and Bruno Leone, eds. *AIDS: Opposing Viewpoints.* San Diego: Greenhaven Press, 1992.

Boyd-Franklin, Nancy, Gloria L. Steiner, and Mary G. Boland, eds. *Children, Families, and HIV/AIDS.* New York: Guilford Press, 1995.

"Care of HIV/AIDS Patients, The." *Military Chaplains' Review,* Spring 1988.

Fortunato, John E. *AIDS: The Spiritual Dilemma.* New York: Harper & Row, 1987.

Gabriel, Martha A. *AIDS Trauma and Support Group Therapy.* Old Tappan, N.J.: The Free Press, 1996.

Greaser, Frances Bontrager. *And a Time to Die.* Scottdale, Pa.: Herald Press, 1995.

Hendrickson, Peter A. *Alive and Well: A Path for Living in a Time of HIV*. New York: Irvington Publishers, 1991.

Kalichman, Seth C. *Preventing AIDS: A Sourcebook for Behavioral Interventions*. Mahwah, N.J.: Lawrence Erlbaum Associates, 1998.

Koop, C. Everett, and Timothy Johnson. *Let's Talk*. Grand Rapids: Zondervan, 1992.

Kübler-Ross, Elisabeth. *AIDS: The Ultimate Challenge*. Old Tappan, N.J.: Macmillan, 1987.

Landau-Stanton, Judith, Colleen D. Clements, et al. *AIDS: Health and Mental Health*. New York: Brunner/Mazel Publishers, 1993.

Shelp, Earl E., and Roland H. Sunderland. *AIDS and the Church*. Louisville: Westminster, 1987.

Sontag, Susan. *AIDS and Its Metaphors*. New York: Farrer, Straus, and Giroux, 1988.

Videos from Mennonite Central Committee (MCC), 21 S. 12th St., Akron, PA 17501-0500 (717-859-3889; fax: 717-859-3875):
Adolescents at Risk for HIV Infection. (22 min.).
AIDS and the Church: Crisis or Opportunity? (27 min.).
Belinda. (29 min.). On HIV and a person's experience.
Going Home: A Family Facing AIDS. (30 min.).
HIV in the Workplace: Prevention and Management of Occupational Exposure to HIV. (15 min.).

Cross-Gender Friendship

Bustanoby, Andre. *Can Men and Women Be Just Friends?* rev. ed. Grand Rapids: Zondervan, 1993.

Joyce, Mary Rosera. *How Can a Man and Woman Be Friends?* Collegeville, Minn.: Liturgical Press, 1977.

Kennedy, Eugene C. *On Being a Friend*. New York: Continuum Pub. Co., 1982.

Gender Roles

Baxter, Anne, and Nora O. Lozano-Diaz, eds. *Woman's Work*. Scottdale, Pa.: Herald Press, 1994.

Beal, Carole R. *Boys and Girls: The Development of Gender Roles*. New York: McGraw-Hill, 1994.

Kanyoro, Musimbi. "Sitting Down Together." *The Other Side* 34/3 (May/June, 1998): 36-39.

Lieb, Frank B. *Friendly Competitors, Fierce Companions: Men's Ways of Relating*. Cleveland: Pilgrim Press, 1997.

Petrikin, Jonathan S. *Male/Female Roles*. Opposing Viewpoints Series. San Diego: Greenhaven Press, 1995.

Penner, Carol, ed. *Women and Men: Gender in the Church*. Scottdale, Pa.: Herald Press, 1998.

Infertility

MCC Women's Concerns Report Nov./Dec. 1996. On infertility.

Richardson, Jill M. "When the Sun Doesn't Shine on Mother's Day." *Christian Living* 41/3 (April/May 1994): 20-21.

Salzer, Linda P. *Surviving Infertility*. New York: Harper Perennial, 1991.

Shapiro, Constance Hoenk. *Infertility and Pregnancy Loss*. San Francisco: Jossey-Bass, 1988.

Simons, Harriet Fishman. *Wanting Another Child: Coping with Secondary Infertility*. Lexington, Mass.: Lexington Books, 1995.

Zoldbrod, Aline P. *Men, Women, and Infertility*. Lexington, Mass.: Lexington Books, 1993.

Intimacy

Abbott, F. *Men and Intimacy*. Freedom, Calif.: Crossing Press, 1990.

Dawn, Marva J. *Sexual Character: Beyond Technique to Intimacy*. Grand Rapids: Eerdmans, 1993.

Nelson, James B. *The Intimate Connection: Male Sexuality, Masculine Spirituality*. Louisville: Westminster, 1988.

Smalley, Gary, and John Trent. *The Two Sides of Love*. Pomona, Calif.: Focus on the Family, 1990.

Smedes, Lewis B. *Love Within Limits*. Grand Rapids: Eerdmans, 1978.

Stafford, Tim. *The Sexual Christian*. Wheaton, Ill.: Victor Books, 1984.

Storkey, Elaine. *The Search for Intimacy*. Grand Rapids: Eerdmans, 1996.

Marriage

Ayo, Nicholas, and Meinrad Craighead. *Sacred Marriage: The Wisdom of the Song of Songs*. New York: Continuum Pub. Co., 1997.

Cutrer, William, and Sandra Glahn. *Sexual Intimacy in Marriage*. Grand Rapids: Kregel Pubns., 1998.

Gady, C. Welton. *Adultery and Grace: The Ultimate Scandal*. Grand Rapids: Eerdmans, 1996.

Markman, Howard, et al. *Fighting for Your Marriage: Positive Steps for Preventing Divorce and Preserving a Lasting Love*. San Francisco: Jossey-Bass, 1994.

Penner, Clifford L., and Joyce J. Penner. *Fifty-two Ways to Have Fun, Fantastic Sex: A Guidebook for Married Couples.* Nashville: Thomas Nelson, 1994.

_____. *Getting Your Sex Life Off to a Great Start: A Guide for Engaged and Newlywed Couples.* Dallas: Word, Inc., 1994.

_____. *Men and Sex: Discovering Greater Love, Passion, and Intimacy with Your Wife.* Nashville: Thomas Nelson, 1997.

Rousseau, Mary, and Charles Gallagher. *Sexual Healing in Marriage.* New York: Continuum Pub. Co., 1994.

Scott, Kieran, and Michael Warren, eds. *Perspectives on Marriage: A Reader.* New York: Oxford Univ. Press, 1993.

Smith, Earl, and Rose Smith. *Sizzling Monogamy.* Albuquerque: William Havens, 1997.

Stahmann, Robert F., and William J. Hiebert. *Premarital and Remarital Counseling: The Professional's Handbook.* San Francisco: Jossey-Bass, 1997.

Vogt, Ron, and Laurie Vogt. "Warning Signs of Marital Distress." *Christian Living* 42/3 (April/May 1995): 13-16.

Same-Sex Orientation

Augsburger, Myron. "Futurism and Anabaptist Mennonites." *Christian Living,* 45/4 (June 1998): 2.

Biesecker-Mast, Gerald J. "Mennonite Public Discourse and the Conflicts over Homosexuality." *Mennonite Quarterly Review* 72/2 (Apr. 1998); 275-300.

Dawson Scanzoni, Letha. "Called to a New Land: Answering Some Questions, Part I." *Daughters of Sarah* 14/3 (May/June 1988): 35-37.

_____. "Responses and Connections: Answering Some Questions, Part II." *Daughters of Sarah* 14/5 (Sept./Oct. 1988): 15-17.

Fortunato, John E. *Embracing the Exile: Healing Journeys of Gay Christians.* New York: HarperCollins, 1982.

Gomes, Peter J. "The Bible and Homosexuality: The Last Prejudice." In *The Good Book: Reading the Bible with Mind and Heart.* New York: Wm. Morrow, 1996, 144-172.

Grenz, Stanley J. *Welcoming but Not Affirming: An Evangelical Response to Homosexuality.* Louisville: Westminster John Knox, 1998.

Hays, Richard B. "Homosexuality." In *The Moral Vision of the New Testament: A Contemporary Introduction to New Testament Ethics.* San Francisco: HarperSanFrancisco, 1996, 379-406.

Hestenes, Roberta. "Reconciliation: Loving Our Way to the Light." *Christian Living* 41/7 (Oct./Nov. 1994): 22-23.

"Homosexuality." *Journal of Psychology and Christianity* 15/4 (Winter 1996): entire journal.

Kreider, Roberta Showalter, ed. *From Wounded Hearts.* Gaithersburg, Md.: Chi Rho Press, 1998.

Marcus, Eric. *Is It a Choice? Answers to 300 of the Most Frequently Asked Questions About Gays and Lesbians.* San Francisco: Harper-SanFrancisco, 1993.

Marty, Martin E. "The Ultimate Test: Americans Fail to Tolerate Homosexuality." *Park Ridge Center Bulletin* 4 (May/June 1998): 19.

MCC Women's Concerns Report. July/Aug. 1998. On same-sex orientation.

Mickey, Paul A. *Of Sacred Worth.* Nashville: Abingdon, 1991.

Morrison, Melanie. *The Grace of Coming Home: Spirituality, Sexuality, and the Struggle for Justice.* Cleveland: Pilgrim Press, 1995.

White, Mel. *Stranger at the Gate: To Be Gay and Christian in America.* New York: Plume, 1995.

Sexual Abuse: Printed Resources

Allender, Dan B. *The Wounded Heart: Hope for Adult Victims of Childhood Sexual Abuse.* Nav Press, 1992.

Angelica, Jade C. *A Moral Emergency: Breaking the Cycle of Child Sexual Abuse.* Kansas City, Mo.: Sheed and Ward, 1993.

Bass, Ellen, and Laura Davis. *The Courage to Heal: A Guide for Women Survivors of Child Sexual Abuse.* 3d ed. New York: HarperCollins, 1994.

Bean, Barbara, and Shari Bennett. *A Guide for Teen Survivors: The Me Nobody Knows.* Lexington, Mass.: Lexington Books, 1993.

Brown, Joanne Carlson, and Carole R. Bohn, eds. *Christianity, Patriarchy and Abuse: A Feminist Critique.* Cleveland: Pilgrim Press, 1989.

Brown Douglas, Kelly. "Daring to Speak." *The Other Side* 34/3 (May/June 1998): 16-17.

Center for the Prevention of Sexual and Domestic Violence. 1914 N. 34th St., Suite 105, Seattle, WA 98103-9058 (206-634-1903; fax: 206-634-0115).

Davies, Jody Messler, and Mary Gail Frawley. *Treating the Adult Survivor of Childhood Sexual Abuse: A Psychoanalytic Perspective.* New York: Basic Books, HarperCollins, 1994.

Davis, Laura. *Allies in Healing: When the Person You Love Was Sexually Abused as a Child.* New York: Harper Perennial, 1991.

Draucker, Claire Burke. *Counseling Survivors of Childhood Sexual Abuse.* London: Sage, 1992.

Feldmeth, Joanne Ross, and Midge Wallace Finley. *We Weep for Ourselves and Our Children: A Christian Guide for Survivors of Childhood Sexual Abuse*. San Francisco: Harper & Row, 1991.

Fortune, Marie M. *Love Does No Harm: Sexual Ethics for the Rest of Us*. New York: Continuum Pub. Co., 1995.

Glaser, Danya, and Stephen Frosh. 2d ed. *Child Sexual Abuse*. Toronto: Univ. of Toronto Press, 1993.

Heggen, Carolyn Holderread. *Sexual Abuse in Christian Homes and Churches*. Scottdale, Pa.: Herald Press, 1993.

Hunter, Mic. *Abused Boys: The Neglected Victims of Sexual Abuse*. New York: Fawcett Book Group, 1990.

Keene, Jane A. *A Winter's Song: A Liturgy for Women Seeking Healing from Sexual Abuse in Childhood*. Cleveland: Pilgrim Press, 1991.

Lew, Mike. *Victims No Longer: Men Recovering From Incest and Other Child Sexual Abuse*. New York: Harper & Row, 1988.

Mennonite Central Committee (MCC) packets. MCC U.S. Women's Concerns, 21 S. 12th St., PO Box 500, Akron, PA 17501-0500 (717-859-3889; fax: 717-859-3875):

"Broken Boundaries: Child Sexual Abuse." Resources for Pastoring People. 1989.

"Crossing the Boundary: Sexual Abuse by Professionals." 1990.

"Expanding the Circle of Caring: Ministering to the Family Members of Survivors and Perpetrators of Sexual Abuse." 1995.

"Lord, Hear Our Prayers." Domestic Violence Worship Resources. 1994.

"Purple Packet: Wife Abuse." Domestic Violence Resources for Pastoring Persons. 1987.

Nafziger-Meiser, Linda. *From Crescent to Circle: A Survivors' Liturgy for Worship, Grief, and Hope*. Elkhart, IN 46515-1245: Mennonite Board of Congregational Ministries (219-294-7523), 1994.

Palmer, Parker J. *The Courage to Teach: Exploring the Inner Landscape of a Teacher's Life*. San Francisco: Jossey-Bass, 1998.

Pellauer, Mary D., et al., eds. *Sexual Assault and Abuse: A Handbook for Clergy and Religious Professionals*. San Francisco: Harper, 1991.

Poston, Carol, and Karen Lison. *Reclaiming Our Lives*. New York: Bantam Books, 1990.

"Pastoral Sexual Abuse." *MCC Conciliation Quarterly* 10/2 (Fall 1991): a report.

Reid, Kathryn Goering, and Marie M. Fortune. *Preventing Child Sexual Abuse: Ages 9-12*. Cleveland: Pilgrim Press, 1989.

Roy, Rustum. "Can Christians Like Sex?" *The Other Side* 34/3 (May/June 1998): 18-19.

Schroeder, Celeste S. *Embodied Prayer: Harmonizing Body and Soul.* Liguori, Mo.: Liguori Press, 1995.

"This Is My Body: A Response to Prostitution." *Daughters of Sarah,* Winter 1993.

Trepper, Terry S., and Mary Jo Barrett. *Systemic Treatment of Incest: A Therapeutic Handbook.* New York: Brunner/Mazel Pubs., 1989.

Trobisch, Walter. *The Complete Works of Walter Trobisch.* Downers Grove, Ill.: InterVarsity Press, 1987.

Ward, Hannah, and Jennifer Wild. *Human Rites: Worship Resources for an Age of Change.* London: Mobray, 1995.

Warshaw, Robin. *I Never Called It Rape: The Ms. Report on Recognizing, Fighting, and Surviving Date and Acquaintance Rape.* Repr. ed. New York: Harper Perennial, 1994.

Westerlund, Elaine. *Women's Sexuality After Childhood Incest.* New York: W. W. Norton & Co., 1992.

Yantzi, Mark. *Sexual Offending and Restoration.* Scottdale, Pa.: Herald Press, 1998.

Sexual Abuse: Video Resources

Inner Voice of Child Abuse, The. Exploration of psychological dynamics underlying physical and emotional abuse of children, demonstrated through interviews with parents who abuse their children. Psychological and Educational Films (714-494-5079).

Little Bear. A children's story told from the point of view of Little Bear, who is molested by an adult. Bridgework Theatre, 113 1/2 E. Lincoln Ave., Goshen, IN 46526 (219-534-1085).

MCC Resource Catalog, The (1997-98) Lists videos on sexual issues, available from MCC, 21 S. 12th St., PO Box 500, Akron, PA 17501-0500 (717-859-3889):

After Sexual Abuse. A two-part video (52 min.).

Ask Before You Hug: Sexual Harassment in the Church (31 min.).

Beyond the News: Sexual Abuse (21 min.).

Hear Their Cries: Religious Responses to Child Abuse (48 min.).

Naked and Uncensored: A Counterfeit Love Story. On pornography (30 min.).

Room Full of Men, A: Male Violence to Women (48 min.).

No More Secrets. A therapist discusses incest, and women and men tell their stories of abuse. ASK (Abused Survivors Know), PO Box 323, Vienna, VA 22183 (703-281-7468).

Not in My Church. Lombard Mennonite Peace Center, 528 E. Madison, Lombard, IL 60148-3599 (708-627-5310).

Sexual Abuse in Christian Homes and Churches. Mennonite Media Productions (800-999-3534).

Summer's Story: The Truth and Trauma of Date Rape. The story of a young woman who is raped by a college acquaintance. Santa Fe Rape Crisis Center, PO Box 116346, Santa Fe, NM 87502 (505-986-9111).

Why, God—Why Me? "I became two people. The little girl who could step out of my body, and the little girl that had to go up the stairs with him. That other little girl didn't hurt or cry." Varied Directions, 69 Elm St., Camden, ME 04843 (207-236-8506).

Sexuality and Aging

Butler, Robert N., and Myrna I. Lewis. *Love and Sex After 60.* Rev. ed. New York: Harper & Row, 1988.

Fanning, Marilyn. "Fifty Years and Still in Love." *Christian Living* 43/5 (Summer 1996): 14-16.

Slabach, Gertrude M. "I Want to Grow Old with You." *Christian Living* 43/1 (Winter 1996): 18-20.

Walz, Thomas H., and Nancee S. Blum. *Sexual Health in Later Life.* Lexington, Mass.: D.C. Heath & Co., 1987.

Sexuality Education

Baldwin, S., and M. Baranoski. "Family Interaction and Sex Education in the Home." *Adolescence* 25 (1990): 573-582.

Bird, Lewis P., and Christopher Reilly. *Learning to Love: A Guide to Sex Education Through the Church.* Waco, Tex.: Word, Inc., 1971.

Brock, L. J., and G. H. Jennings. (1993). "What Daughters in Their 30s Wish Their Mothers Had Told Them." *Family Relations* 42/1 (1993): 61-65.

Byer, Curtis O., Lewis W. Shainberg, and Grace Galliano. *Dimensions of Human Sexuality.* 5th ed. New York: McGraw-Hill College Div., 1998.

Clapp, Steve. *Teenage Sexuality: Local Church and Christian Home Program Guide.* Champaign, Ill.: C-4 (Christ, Change, Community, and Covenant) Resources, 1985.

Clapp, Steve, Sue Brownfield, and Julie Seibert. Champaign, Ill.: C-4 (Christ, Change, Community, and Covenant) Resources:
A Christian View of Youth and Sexuality. 1982.
Dating, Marriage, and Sexuality: An Adult Guide. 1986.
Dating, Marriage, and Sexuality: A Guide for Christian Youth. 1986.

Drolet, J., and K. Clark, eds. *The Sexuality Education Challenge: Promoting Healthy Sexuality in Young People.* Santa Cruz, Calif.: ETR Associates, 1994.

Harris, E. "How to Talk to Your Children About Sexuality and Other Important Issues: A SIECUS Annotated Bibliography for Parents." *SIECUS Report* 22/3 (1994): 18-20.

Maksym, D. *Shared Feelings: A Parent Guide to Sexuality Education for Children, Adolescents, and Adults Who Have a Mental Handicap.* North York, Ont.: G. Allan Roeher Inst., 1990.

Presbyterian Church USA and Reformed Church in America. *God's Gift of Sexuality* (6 sessions for grades 5-8, and 10 sessions for grades 9-12): *God's Plan for Growing Up Wonderfully Made* (grades 2-3); *Amazing Stuff* (grades 4-5); *Listening In* (audiotape to help parents talk with their children about sexuality). Presbyterian Publishing House, 100 Witherspoon St., Louisville, KY 40202 (800-227-2872).

Rizzo Toner, P. *Relationships and Communication Activities.* (Includes 90 ready-to-use worksheets for grades 7-12). West Nyack, N.Y.: Center for Applied Research in Education, 1993.

Unitarian Universalist Association and United Church of Christ Board for Homeland Ministries. *Our Whole Lives: A Lifespan Sexuality Education Series.* United Church of Christ Board for Homeland Ministries, 700 Prospect Ave., Cleveland, OH 44115 (216-736-3282). 1999.

Weston, Carol. *Girltalk: All the Stuff Your Sister Never Told You.* 3d ed. New York: Harper Perennial, 1997.

Sexuality and Theology

Arnold, William V. *Pastoral Responses to Sexual Issues.* Louisville: Westminster John Knox, 1993.

Cahill, Lisa Sowle. *Between the Sexes: Foundations for a Christian Ethics of Sexuality.* Philadelphia: Fortress, 1985.

_____. *Sex, Gender and Christian Ethics.* Cambridge: Cambridge Univ. Press, 1996.

Charles, Howard. "Sexuality in the New Testament." Unpublished paper, 1984 (available from author: 219-533-8444).

Countryman, L. William. *Dirt, Greed, and Sex: Sexual Ethics in the New Testament and Their Implications for Today.* Philadelphia: Fortress, 1988.

Davidson, Doug. "Roots and Branches: An Embodied Faith." *The Other Side* 34/3 (1998): 46.

Doniger, Wendy. "Sexuality and Religion: Divine Marriage or Divine Alchemy." *Park Ridge Center Bulletin* 4 (May/June 1998): 17.

Eugene, Toinette M. "Faithful Responses to Human Sexuality: Issues Facing the Church Today." *Chicago Theological Seminary Register,* Spring 1991, 1-7.

Gill, Margaret. *Free to Love: Sexuality and Pastoral Care*. New York: HarperCollins, 1994.

Green, Ronald M., ed. *Religion and Sexual Health: Ethical, Theological and Clinical Perspectives*. Norwell, Mass.: Kluwer, 1992.

Gudorf, Christine E. *Body, Sex and Pleasure: Reconstructing Christian Sexual Ethics*. Cleveland: Pilgrim Press, 1994.

Hahn, Celia Alison. *Sexual Paradox: Creative Tensions in Our Lives and in Our Congregations*. New York: Pilgrim Press, 1991.

Heyward, Carter. *Touching Our Strength: The Erotic as Power and the Love of God*. New York: HarperCollins, 1989.

Hull, C. M. Kathleen, and Wendy Kroeker. *Braiding Hearts and Hands: A Poetry and Dramatic Arts Anthology*. Winnipeg: Mennonite Central Committee Canada, 1994.

Mennonite Church and General Conference Mennonite Church. *Human Sexuality in the Christian Life*. Newton, Kan.: Faith & Life, 1985.

Moltmann-Wendell, Elisabeth. *I Am My Body: A Theology of Embodiment*. New York: Continuum Pub. Co., 1995.

Nelson, James B. *Body Theology*. Louisville: Westminster, 1992.

_____. *Embodiment: An Approach to Sexuality and Christian Theology*. Minneapolis: Augsburg, 1978.

Nelson, James B., and Sandra P. Longfellow, eds. *Sexuality and the Sacred: Sources for Theological Reflection*. Louisville: Westminster, 1994.

O'Connell, Laurence J. "Human Sexuality: Important Intersection of Health, Faith, and Ethics." *Park Ridge Center Bulletin* 4 (May/June 1998): 2.

Penner, Clifford L., and Joyce J. Penner. *The Gift of Sex: A Christian Guide to Sexual Fulfillment*. Waco, Tex.: Word, Inc., 1981.

_____. *Counseling for Sexual Disorders*. Dallas: Word, Inc., 1990.

Rousseau, Mary, and Charles Gallagher. *Sex Is Holy*. New York: Continuum Pub. Co., 1986.

Smedes, Lewis B. *Sex for Christians: The Limits and Liberties of Sexual Living*. Grand Rapids: Eerdmans, 1992.

Thomas, Zach. *Healing Touch: The Church's Forgotten Language*. Louisville: Westminster, 1995.

Wiens, Delbert. "Propriety, Purity, and Partnership." *The Other Side* 34/3 (May/June 1998): 14-17.

Sexuality in Illness and Disability

Carroll, Janell L., and Paul Root Wolpe. "Sexuality in Illness and Disability." *Sexuality and Gender in Society*. 3d ed. New York: HarperCollins College Pub., 1996, 473-491.

Kelly, Gary F. "Sex and Disability Groups." *Sexuality Today: The Human Perspective.* 6th ed. New York: McGraw-Hill, 1998, 229-237.

Sexual Misconduct by Clergy

Fortune, Marie M. *Is Nothing Sacred? When Sex Invades the Pastoral Relationship.* San Francisco: HarperSanFrancisco, 1989.

_____. "Betrayal of the Pastoral Relationship: Sexual Contact by Pastors and Pastoral Counselors." In Gary Schoener, et al. *Psychotherapists Sexual Involvement with Clients: Intervention and Prevention.* Minneapolis: Walk-In Counseling Center, 1989.

Keene, Jane A. "By God Betrayed?" *The Other Side* 26/1 (Jan./Feb. 1990): 24-27.

Lebacqz, Karen, and Ronald G. Barton. *Sex in the Parish.* Louisville: Westminster John Knox, 1991.

Mennonite Central Committee U.S. Peace Section. "Pastoral Sexual Misconduct: The Church's Response." *Conciliation Quarterly Newsletter* 10/2 (Spring 1991).

Rediger, G. Lloyd. *Ministry and Sexuality: Cases, Counseling, and Care.* Minneapolis: Fortress, 1990.

Rutter, Peter. *Sex in the Forbidden Zone.* Los Angeles: Jeremy P. Torcher, 1989.

Washington Association of Churches. *The Church's Responsibility for the Safety of Children, Youth, and Vulnerable Adults.* Seattle, 1991.

Wilson, Earl and Sandy, Paul and Virginia Friesen, Larry and Paul Paulson. *Restoring the Fallen: A Team Approach to Caring, Confronting, and Reconciling.* Downers Grove. Ill.: InterVarsity Press, 1997.

Singleness

Beslow, Audrey. *Sex and the Single Christian.* Nashville: Abingdon, 1987.

Brubaker, Shirley Yoder. "One Is a Whole Number." *The Mennonite* 1/14 (May 26, 1998): 8-10.

Goergen, Donald. *The Sexual Celibate.* New York: Seabury, 1974.

Martin, Mariann. "Ten Questions to Ask a Single Person Other Than . . ." *The Mennonite* 1/14 (May 26, 1998): 11.

MCC Women's Concerns Report. Mar./Apr. 1994. On single women.

Withers, Richard. "Beloved of God." *The Other Side* 34/3 (May/June 1998): 20-29.

Notes

1. The Gift

Fairlie, Henry. "Lust or Luxuria." *New Republic* 177 (Oct. 8, 1977): 18-21.

Goergen, Donald. *The Sexual Celibate*. New York: Seabury Press, 1974.

Nelson, James B. *Embodiment: An Approach to Sexuality and Christian Theology*. Minneapolis: Augsburg, 1978.

Nelson, James B., and Sandra P. Longfellow, eds. *Sexuality and the Sacred: Sources for Theological Reflection*. Louisville: Westminster John Knox, 1994.

Warren, Neil Clark. On back cover of *Sex for Christians*, by Lewis B. Smedes. Grand Rapids: Eerdmans, 1992.

2. Guidelines from the Gift-Giver

Cahill, Lisa Sowle. *Between the Sexes: Foundations for a Christian Ethics of Sexuality*. Philadelphia: Fortress Press, 1985.

_____. *Sex, Gender and Christian Ethics*. Cambridge: Cambridge Univ. Press, 1996.

Charles, Howard. "Sexuality in the New Testament." Unpublished paper, 1984.

Kazantzakis, Nikos. *The Last Temptation of Christ*. New York: Simon & Schuster Trade, Touchstone, 1971, 1998 repr.

Mennonite Church and General Conference Mennonite Church. *Human Sexuality in the Christian Life*. Newton, Kan.: Faith & Life Press, 1985.

Nelson, James B., and Sandra P. Longfellow, eds. See under chap. 1, above.

Smedes, Lewis B. *Sex for Christians*. Grand Rapids: Eerdmans, 1992.

Stoltzfus, Edward "Biblical Perspectives on Sexuality." Unpublished and undated paper.

Yoder, Perry, and Elizabeth Yoder. *New Men—New Roles*. Newton, Kan.: Faith & Life Press, 1977.

3. The Gift and Intimacy

Bauman, Harold. Goshen College campus pastor, 1958-1974.

Cooper, Rod. *New Man*, Mar./Apr. 1995.

Gilligan, Carol. *In a Different Voice*. Cambridge: Harvard Univ. Press, 1982.

Landers, Ann. *Chicago Tribune*, Jan. 24, 1985; Nov. 1995.

Rubin, Lillian. *Intimate Strangers: Men and Women Together*. New York: Harper & Row, 1983.

4. The Gift and Young People

Carrera, Michael A. "Adolescent Sexuality: Looking Above the Waist." In *Lessons for Lifeguards: Working with Teens When the Topic Is Hope.* PO Box 20583, New York 10021-0071: Donkey Press, 1996.

Corning, Susan, and Charlotte Noyes. "The Battle for Teen Health: What's Worked and What It Tells Us." *Trustee,* Mar. 1997, 23-25.

National Campaign to Prevent Teen Pregnancy. "Ten Tips for Parents to Help Their Children Avoid Teen Pregnancy." *Campaign Update,* Summer 1998, 4.

5. The Gift and Singleness

Cartlidge, D. "1 Corinthians 7 as a Foundation for a Christian Sex Ethic." *The Journal of Religion* 55/2 (Apr. 1975): 322-323.

Goergen, Donald. *The Sexual Celibate.* New York: Seabury Press, 1974.

Masters, William H., and Virginia E. Johnson. *The Pleasure Bond: A New Look at Sexuality and Commitment.* Boston: Little, Brown, & Co., 1974.

Mennonite Church and General Conference Mennonite Church. "Singleness." In *Human Sexuality in the Christian Life.* Newton, Kan.: Faith & Life, 1985, 59-65, 74-79.

White, Bill. *Tabletalk.* Ligonier Valley Study Center, 564 North Lake Blvd., Altamonte Springs, FL 32701, 1980.

6. The Gift and Marriage

Axinn, W. G., and A. Thornton. "The Relationship Between Cohabitation and Divorce: Selectivity or Casual Influence?" *Demography,* 1992, 29, 357-374.

Charles, Howard. "Sexuality in the New Testament." In section "Toward Some Basic New Testament Guidelines." Goshen, Ind.: Unpublished paper, 1984.

Rathus, Spencer A., Jeffrey S. Nevid, and Lois Fischner-Rathus. *Human Sexuality in a World of Diversity.* 3rd ed. Boston: Allyn & Bacon, 1997.

Rosen, Rosanne. *The Living Together Trap.* Far Hills, N.J.: New Horizon Press, 1993.

Sider, Arbutus, and Ron Sider. "Wedded Witness." *Prism,* Sept./Oct. 1995.

Smedes, Lewis B. *Sex for Christians.* Grand Rapids: Eerdmans, 1992.

U.S. National Center for Health Statistics. *New York Times,* Oct. 5, 1996.

7. The Gift and Same-Sex Orientation

Augsburger, Myron. "Futurism and Anabaptist Mennonites." *Christian Living* 45/4 (June 1998): 2.

Bird, Lewis P. Address at Goshen College, Mar. 4, 1982, in "Sexuality Week."

Gomes, Peter J. *The Good Book: Reading the Bible with Mind and Heart.* New York: Wm. Morrow, 1996.

Grenz, Stanley J. *Welcoming but Not Affirming: An Evangelical Response to Homosexuality.* Louisville: Westminster John Knox, 1998.

Hays, Richard B. "Homosexuality." In *The Moral Vision of the New Testament: A Contemporary Introduction to New Testament Ethics.* San Francisco: HarperSanFrancisco, 1996, 379-406.

Headings, Verle. "Etiology of Homosexuality." *Southern Medical Journal* 73/8 (Aug. 1980): 1024-1030.

Kinsey, A. C., et al. *Sexual Behavior in the Human Female*. Philadelphia: W. B. Saunders, 1953.

Mennonite Church and General Conference Mennonite Church. *Human Sexuality in the Christian Life*. Newton, Kan.: Faith & Life Press, 1985.

Rohr, Richard. "Sexuality: The Search for Wholeness." Audiotaped presentation. Cincinnati: St. Anthony Messenger Tapes.

Smedes, Lewis B. *Sex for Christians*. Grand Rapids: Eerdmans, 1992.

Taylor, Daniel. "Confessions of a Bible Translator." *Christianity Today* 41/12 (Oct. 27, 1997): 76-77.

Yancey, Philip. "And the Word Was . . . Debatable." *Christianity Today* 42/6 (May 18, 1998): 88.

8. The Gift and Cross-Gender Friendships

Joyce, Mary Rosera. *How Can a Man and Woman Be Friends?* Collegeville, Minn.: Liturgical Press, 1977.

Kennedy, Eugene C. *On Being a Friend*. New York: Continuum, 1982.

9. The Gift and the Sensuous

SC Communications. *The Sexiest Animal*. 1990. 37-min. video. Wombat Film & Video, 93 Pitner Avenue, Evanston, IL 60202 (800-323-5448).

Smith, Earl, and Rose Smith. *Sizzling Monogamy*. Albuquerque: Wm. Havens Publishing, 1997.

10. The Gift Expressed in the Arts

Breslin, J. G. *Mark Rothko: A Biography*. Chicago: Univ. of Chicago Press, 1994.

Croce, Benedetto. *The Essence of Aesthetics*. London: Heinemann, 1922.

Danto, Arthur. *Transfiguration of the Common Place: A Philosophy of Art*. Cambridge: Harvard Univ. Press, 1981.

Francoeur, Robert T. *Becoming a Sexual Person*. New York: John Wiley and Sons, 1982.

Hugo, Victor. *The Hunchback of Notre Dame*. New York: Dodd, Mead, and Co., 1947.

Kant, Immanuel. *Critique of Judgement*. 1790 ed. trans. J. H. Bernard. New York: Hafner Press, 1951.

Kermode, Frank. *History and Value*. Oxford: Clarendon, 1988.

Langer, Susanne K. *Philosophy in a New Key*. Cambridge: Harvard Univ. Press, 1978.

Levertov, Denise. *Sand of the Well*. San Francisco: New Directions, 1994.

Nussbaum, Martha. *The Therapy of Desire*. Princeton: Princeton Univ. Press, 1994.

Polanyi, Michael. *The Tacit Dimension*. New York: Peter Smith, 1966.

Smith, Anna Deavere. *Twilight: Los Angeles 1992*. New York: Anchor Books, 1994.

11. The Gift Misused

Alan Guttmacher Institute. "Facts in Brief." New York and Washington, D.C., 1994.

Clapp, Rodney. "Why the Devil Takes VISA." *Christianity Today,* Oct. 7, 1996, 19-33.

C & M Promotions. Computer Internet, May 1998.

Gottman, John. *New York Times,* May 28, 1997.

Gushee, David P. "Divorce: Learning from Farmer Gachet." *Prism*, Sept./Oct. 1995, 18-19.

Hunt, Joan, and Richard Hunt. *Affirming Sexuality in Christian Adulthood.* Nashville, Tenn.: Graded Press, 1982.

Kelly, Gary F. *Sexuality Today: The Human Perspective.* 6th ed. Boston: McGraw-Hill Companies, 1998.

Koop, C. Everett. Oral statement.

Lorde, Audre. "Uses of the Erotic: The Erotic as Power." In *Sexuality and the Sacred: Sources for Theological Reflection,* 75-79. Ed. James B. Nelson and Sandra P. Longfellow. Louisville: Westminster John Knox, 1994.

Marty, Martin E. "M.E.M.O.: Our Own Worst Enemies." *Christian Century*, Sept. 21-28, 1994, 879.

Maynard, Rebecca A., ed. *Kids Having Kids: A Robin Hood Foundation Special Report on the Costs of Adolescent Childbearing.* New York: Robin Hood Foundation, 1996.

Merton, Thomas. "Love and Need: Is Love a Package or a Message?" In *Love and Living: Thomas Merton.* Ed. Naomi Burton Stone and Brother Patrick Hart. New York: Farrar, Straus, and Giroux, 1979.

Nelson, James B. Lecture at Goshen College, Nov. 4, 1997.

Pellauer, Mary D. "Pornography: An Agenda for the Churches." In *Sexuality and the Sacred: Sources for Theological Reflection,* 345-353. Ed. James B. Nelson and Sandra P. Longfellow. Louisville: Westminster John Knox, 1994.

Sider, Arbutus, and Ron Sider. "Wedded Witness." *Prism*, Sept./Oct. 1995.

Storkey, Elaine. *The Search for Intimacy.* Grand Rapids: Eerdmans, 1996.

Wallace, Robert Jr. "'Tween Twelve and Twenty." *Goshen News,* Aug. 11, 1997.

12. The Gift Restored

Center for the Prevention of Sexual and Domestic Violence, 1914 N. 34th St., Suite 105, Seattle, WA 98103-9058 (206-634-1903; fax: 206-634-0115).

Draucker, Claire Burke. *Counseling Survivors of Childhood Sexual Abuse.* London: Sage, 1992.

Eugene, Toinette M. "Faithful Responses to Human Sexuality: Issues Facing the Church Today." *Chicago Theological Seminary Register*, Spring 1991, 1-7.

Fortunato, John E. *Embracing the Exile: Healing Journeys of Gay Christians.* New York: Harper Collins, 1982.

Heggen, Carolyn Holderread. *Sexual Abuse in Christian Homes and Churches.* Scottdale, Pa: Herald Press, 1993.

Keene, Jane A. *A Winter's Song: A Liturgy for Women Seeking Healing from*

Sexual Abuse in Childhood. Cleveland: Pilgrim Press, 1991.

Mennonite Central Committee (MCC) packets. Akron, PA 17501-0500 (717-859-3889; fax: 717-859-3875).

"AIDS: A Christian Response." MCC BC, PO Box 2038, Clearbrook, BC V2T 3T8 (604-850-6639), 1991.

Burnett, Kristina Mast. "Crossing the Boundary: Sexual Abuse by Professionals." 1991.

MCC Domestic Violence Task Force. "Broken Boundaries: Child Sexual Abuse." Resources for Pastoring People. 1989.

Thiessen, Esther Epp. "Expanding the Circle of Caring: Ministering to Family Members of Survivors and Perpetrators of Sexual Abuse." 1995.

Mennonite Church and General Conference Mennonite Church. *Human Sexuality in the Christian Life*. Newton, Kan.: Faith & Life Press, 1985.

Nafziger-Meiser, Linda. *From Crescent to Circle: A Survivors' Liturgy for Worship, Grief, and Hope*. Elkhart, IN 46515-1245: Mennonite Board of Congregational Ministries (219-294-7523), 1994.

Nelson, James B. *Embodiment: An Approach to Sexuality and Christian Theology*. Minneapolis: Augsburg, 1978.

Palmer, Parker J. *The Courage to Teach: Exploring the Inner Landscape of a Teacher's Life*. San Francisco: Jossey-Bass, 1998.

"Pastoral Sexual Abuse." *MCC Conciliation Quarterly* 10/2 (Fall 1991).

Presbyterian Church USA and Reformed Church in America. *God's Gift of Sexuality: God's Plan for Growing Up Wonderfully Made; Amazing Stuff; Listening In*. Louisville: Presbyterian Publishing House, 1996.

Rencken, Robert H. *Intervention Strategies for Sexual Abuse*. Alexandria, Va.: American Association for Counseling and Development, 1989.

Schroeder, Celeste S. *Embodied Prayer: Harmonizing Body and Soul*. Liguori, Mo.: Liguori Press, 1995.

Shelton, Charles M. *Adolescent Spirituality: Pastoral Ministry for High School and College Youth*. New York: Crossroads, 1989.

"This Is My Body: A Response to Prostitution." *Daughters of Sarah*, Winter 1993.

Trobisch, Walter. *I Married You*. New York: Harper & Row, 1971.

_____. *The Complete Works of Walter Trobisch*. Downers Grove, Ill.: InterVarsity, 1987.

Unitarian Universalist Association and United Church of Christ Board for Homeland Ministries. *Our Whole Lives: A Lifespan Sexuality Education Series*. Cleveland: UCC Board for Homeland Ministries, 1999.

Ward, Hannah, and Jennifer Wild. *Human Rites: Worship Resources for an Age of Change*. London: Mobray, 1995.

Yantzi, Mark. *Sexual Offending and Restoration*. Scottdale, Pa.: Herald Press, 1998.

Contributing Authors

Anne Krabill Hershberger, R.N., M.S.N., Editor

Anne is associate professor of nursing at Goshen (Ind.) College, where she teaches maternity nursing, human sexuality, and health care ethics. Earlier she taught nursing at Indiana University and the University of Michigan.

She earned a B.S. in nursing degree from Goshen College in 1958 and a master of science in nursing from Wayne State University, Detroit, in 1963. Her post-master's

study has been in the area of bioethics at the Kennedy Institute of Ethics, Georgetown University, Washington, D.C. (1981-1982); and at the University of California-San Francisco (1988-1989).

During her 1996-1997 sabbatical leave in New York City, Anne did further study in sexuality and bioethics at New York University, helped to design and teach an expanded Expectant Parent Education Program for the Morris Heights Birthing Center in the Bronx, and served on the Sexuality Curriculum Committee for the NYC Covenant House.

While living in Washington, in addition to her bioethics studies, Anne also served as health coordinator of the Cities-In-Schools Adolescent Pregnancy Prevention Program. For seven years she served as director and instructor of the Expectant

Parent Education Program at Goshen General Hospital.

Anne edited the book *Ethics and the Educated Person: A Teaching-Learning Resource* (1993). She has written chapters in Tackett and Hunsberger's *Family-Centered Care of Children and Adolescents: Nursing Concepts in Child Health* (1981), and in Miller and Brubaker's *Bioethics and the Beginning of Life* (1990). She has published articles in *Nursing Outlook, Journal of Advanced Nursing, The Mennonite Encyclopedia* (vol. 5), and *Mennonite Medical Messenger,* as well as other articles and book reviews.

She has numerous professional memberships and has served as president of the Indiana State Nurses Association District 12 and of the Mennonite Nurses Association. Anne is a member of Delta Kappa Gamma (Women Educators' Honorary Society) and the Indiana and Elkhart County Healthy Mothers, Healthy Babies. She was awarded a Lilly Endowment, Inc., Open-Faculty Fellowship in 1981; and the Delta Kappa Gamma Harriet Biddle Scholarship in 1972.

Anne Krabill Hershberger and her husband, Abner, are the parents of two daughters. They are members of College Mennonite Church and live in Goshen, Indiana.

Willard S. Krabill, M.D., M.P.H., Primary Author

Willard is now retired and holds the title of college physician and associate professor of health education emeritus at Goshen (Ind.) College. He received his B.A. degree from Goshen College in 1949, and his M.D. degree from Jefferson Medical College, Philadelphia, in 1953.

He practiced family medicine in North Liberty, Indiana. Willard married Grace Hershberger of Goshen, Indiana. From 1955 to 1958 they served with the Mennonite Central Committee in Banmethuot, South Vietnam, at a leprosarium. Upon returning to the United States, he practiced family medicine in Goshen. Later, after doing a residency in obstetrical medicine, he limited his practice to that area.

Willard pioneered the development of expectant parent education and the opportunity for fathers to be present at the birth of their babies at Goshen General Hospital—firsts in the region. In 1972-1973 he earned a master's degree in public health at the University of California, Berkeley. He took an intensive course in bioethics at the Kennedy Institute of Ethics, Georgetown University, Washington, D.C. In 1984 he was a scholar-in-residence at the Institute for Religion and Wholeness, School of Theology at Claremont, California.

In 1967, he became Goshen College physician. During his twenty-four years in that position, he emphasized the importance of each person assuming personal responsibility for her or his own wellness and health education. Willard developed and taught a popular human sexuality course. This was done when such courses were rare, especially on Christian college campuses. In addition, he developed and taught other courses: "Health in a Changing Environment" and "The Use and Abuse of Chemicals."

Throughout his career and into retirement, Willard has been an articulate author, spokesperson, and innovator in the areas of health, wellness, sexuality, substance use and abuse, and bioethics. He holds numerous professional memberships. He has served as president and executive secretary of the Mennonite Medical Association. He has served on the Health and Welfare Committee of the Mennonite Board of Missions and on the Human Sexuality Study Committee of the General Board of the Mennonite Church. He was a medical and bioethics consultant to Mennonite Mutual Aid Association.

His awards include membership in Alpha Omega Alpha (Honorary Medical Society). In 1988 he received the Allen H. Erb Memorial Award from the Mennonite Health Association. He was named Doctor of the Year by the Mennonite Medical Association in 1990. In 1995 he was given the Anabaptist Healthcare Award by Mennonite Mutual Aid Association.

Willard S. Krabill and his wife, Grace, are the parents of four children and have seven grandchildren. They are members of College Mennonite Church and live in Goshen, Indiana.

Delores Histand Friesen, Ph.D.

Delores is associate professor of pastoral counseling at the Mennonite Brethren Biblical Seminary in Fresno, California, where she has taught for ten years in the area of marriage, family, and child counseling. She is a graduate of Hesston College and earned a B.A. in elementary education from Goshen (Ind.) College. Her master's degree in international and comparative education is from Indiana University, and her Ph.D. in counseling and human development is from the University of Iowa.

For three years Delores taught at Parkside Elementary School in Goshen. She and her husband, J. Stanley Friesen, then worked for thirteen years with the Mennonite Board of Missions in theological education with African Independent Churches in West Africa. This is where she began teaching and ministering in the area of human sexuality. She wrote a book on the subject, *Let Love Be Your Greatest* (Editions Trobisch, Kehl, Germany, 1979), translated into several languages.

Other publications include the following: *All Are Witnesses* (Kindred Publications, 1996); editor of a collection of Mennonite Brethren women's sermons; *Living More with Less Study/*

Action Guide (Herald Press, 1981; rev. ed., Alternatives for Simple Living, 1999); chapters in *Healing the Children of War, Growing Towards Peace,* and *A Kingdom of Priests*; Sunday school lessons in *Adult Bible Study*; articles and poetry in magazines such as *Builder, Christian Living, Direction, Christian Leader,* and *Mission Focus.*

She is a licensed marriage, family, and child counselor and maintains a small psychotherapy practice. She has served on the Board of Mennonite Brethren Missions and Services International for five years.

Delores Histand Friesen and her husband, Stan, are the parents of three children and live in Fresno, California. They are members of First Mennonite Church, Iowa City; and College Community Mennonite Brethren Church, Clovis, California.

Lauren Friesen, Ph.D.

Lauren is lecturer in theatre history and director of playwriting at the University of Michigan-Flint. For fifteen years he served as professor of drama and director of the theatre program at Goshen (Ind.) College. He pastored the Seattle Mennonite Church from 1974 to 1980.

His degrees include a B.A. in history and philosophy from Bethel College, Newton, Kansas, in 1967; a master of divinity from Mennonite Biblical Seminary, Elkhart, Indiana, in 1970; an M.A. in religion and the arts from Pacific School of Religion, Berkeley, in 1981; and a Ph.D. in religion and the arts "with distinction" from the Graduate Theological Union in cooperation with the University of California-Berkeley in 1985.

Lauren has published and directed numerous plays and has

published poetry in many journals. For the General Conference Mennonite Church, he served as chair of the Worship and Arts Committee for five years, and chair of the Media Division for four years.

His other professional appointments include serving as chair of The Kennedy Center/American College Theatre Festival Awards Selection Team and chair of Region III; Association for Theatre in Higher Education Playwriting Program judge and dramaturge and chair of the Religion and Theatre Program; vice-president of the Indiana Theatre Association; dramaturge for the New Harmony Media Project (Ind.) for NBC and Walt Disney Studios' writers; and numerous roles in consulting and adjudication.

The most recent of his many awards include The Kennedy Center Medallion for Excellence in University/College Theatre in 1997; the Indiana Theatre Association Outstanding Achievement in University/College Theatre Award in 1997; and Honorable Mention from the Alaska Native American Play Competition for *Hawk Feather* in 1996.

Lauren Friesen and his wife, Janet Burkholder Friesen, are the parents of two children. They are members of College Mennonite Church in Goshen, Indiana, and live in Swartz Creek, Michigan.

Keith Graber Miller, Ph.D.

Keith is associate professor of Bible, religion, and philosophy at Goshen (Ind.) College, teaching in the areas of sexuality, Christian ethics and theology, religion and politics, religious history, and the sociology of religion. He also has been a visiting faculty member at Associated Mennonite Biblical Seminary, Elkhart, Indiana, where he received his master of divinity degree in 1988. He earned his B.A. degree from Franklin College (Ind.) in 1981. He completed his Ph.D. degree in religion at Emory University, Atlanta, in 1993.

Before completing his doctoral work and joining Goshen College's Bible, Religion, and Philosophy Department, Keith served as an assistant professor of communication and interim campus minister at the college; a co-pastor of Howard-Miami Mennonite Church in Kokomo, Indiana; and the editor and general manager of a weekly newspaper, *The Howard County News*.

Keith has published numerous articles in academic journals and has edited texts. His first book, *Wise As Serpents, Innocent As Doves: American Mennonites Engage Washington* (Univ. of Tenn. Press, 1996), was based on his dissertation. Over the past decade, he has also written extensively for Mennonite presses.

For his writing and research, he has received a number of grants and fellowships. Since 1996, he has been a participant in the Lilly Endowment, Inc., Rhodes Consultation on the Future of the Church-Related College.

Keith Graber Miller is married to Ann Graber Miller, and they have two children. They are members of College Mennonite Church and live in Goshen, Indiana.

Michael A. Carrera, Ph.D.

Dr. Carrera, the author of the reprinted chapter "Adolescent Sexuality: Looking Above the Waist," has spent almost forty years in the community, working as an educator with young people and families. As Director of The Children's Aid Society, National Adolescent Sexuality and Pregnancy Prevention Training Center, Dr. Carrera trains staff from agencies interested in implementing his holistic, long-term adolescent pregnancy prevention model.

He has received awards from Advocates for Youth, SIECUS, Columbia University, Planned Parenthood Sexuality Educators of America, and the American Association of Sex Educators,

Counselors, and Therapists (ASSECT).

Dr. Carrera, Thomas Hunter Professor Emeritus at Hunter College, is also an adjunct professor at Mount Sinai Medical School in New York City.

He is the author of a number of books, including *Lessons for Lifeguards: Working with Teens When the Topic Is Hope*, *The Wordsworth Dictionary of Sexual Terms*, and *The Language of Sex: An A to Z Guide*.